"Dares us to discover the unique indivi[   ]....u us to be; one for all, all for One, all for His glory. This book will improve your life immensely!"

—Ken Abraham, coauthor, *Let's Roll*, the *New York Times* best-seller

"For those on the journey of spiritual formation, Marita takes understanding your personality from a biblical perspective to another level. A must-read for anyone seeking to enhance and transform their life."

—Sabrina D. Black, international speaker, counselor, and author, *Can Two Walk Together?*, *Prone to Wander, Help! for Your Leadership*, and *Counseling in African American Communities*

"The perfect book for anyone wanting to apply personality to a spiritually focused environment."

—Carole Lewis, national director, First Place

"Our personality *does* impact our spirituality! We are each unique, and we can approach God as He created us!"

—Pam Farrel, author, *The 10 Best Decisions a Woman Can Make* and *Men Are Like Waffles, Women Are Like Spaghetti*, and codirector, Farrel Communications and Masterful Living Ministries

"Marita's timely book provides a tool for understanding and celebrating our God-given uniqueness as we journey our spiritual path."

—Elaine Wright Colvin, director, Writers Information Network

"Should be required reading for all who work in churches, as well as for the rest of us who need to be more tolerant concerning the spiritual uniqueness of each Christian."
—Janice Elsheimer, speaker and author,
The Creative Call, which received the ECPA Silver Medallion

"Warm personal examples and true-life stories make the Personalities come alive."
—Edna Ellison, author, *Woman to Woman: Preparing Yourself to Mentor* and *Friend to Friend*

"Prepare yourself for some intriguing and life-changing ideas."
—Kathy Collard Miller, speaker and author,
Partly Cloudy with Scattered Worries

Other Books by Marita Littauer

But Lord, I Was Happy Shallow

The Journey to Jesus (coauthored with Florence Littauer)

Love Extravagantly (coauthored with Chuck Noon)

You've Got What It Takes

Come As You Are (coauthored with Betty Southard)

Talking So People Will Listen (coauthored with Florence Littauer)

Getting Along With Almost Anybody (coauthored with Florence Littauer)

Personality Puzzle (coauthored with Florence Littauer)

Too Much Is Never Enough (coauthored with Gaylen Larson)

Giving Back

Homemade Memories

Shades of Beauty (coauthored with Florence Littauer)

Your Spiritual Personality

Using the Strengths of Your Personality
to Deepen Your Relationship with God

Marita Littauer

with Betty Southard

Foreword by Florence Littauer

JOSSEY-BASS
A Wiley Imprint
www.josseybass.com

Published by Jossey-Bass
A Wiley Imprint
989 Market Street, San Francisco, CA 94103-1741   www.josseybass.com

Credits are on page 165.

Jossey-Bass books and products are available through most bookstores. To contact Jossey-Bass directly, call our Customer Care Department within the U.S. at 800-956-7739 or outside the U.S. at 317-572-3986, or fax to 317-572-4002.

Jossey-Bass also publishes its books in a variety of electronic formats. Some content that appears in print may not be available in electronic books.

Library of Congress Cataloging-in-Publication Data

Littauer, Marita.
   Your spiritual personality: using the strengths of your personality to deepen your relationship with God / Marita Littauer; foreword by Florence Littauer.
      p. cm.
   ISBN 0-7879-7308-4 (alk. paper)
   1. Personality—Religious aspects—Christianity.   2. Spirituality—Psychology.   I.   Title.
BV4597.57.L58 2004
248.4—dc22   2004010437

Printed in the United States of America
FIRST EDITION
HB Printing   10 9 8 7 6 5 4 3 2 1

Contents

Foreword by Florence Littauer   ix

Part One: What Is My Spiritual Personality?   1

1.   The Spiritual Life of a "Good" Christian   3
2.   The Sonshine Church   15
3.   What Is My Spiritual Personality?   23

Part Two: How Does My Spiritual Personality Affect My Spiritual Life?   37

4.   View of God   39
5.   Worship Experience   51
6.   Spiritual Strength   63
7.   Growing Closer to God   77
8.   The Personality of Jesus   97
9.   Spiritual Personality and Spiritual Gifts   111
10. Encouragement and Freedom   129

Appendix A: Personality Testing Instrument   141
Appendix B: Personality Profile Word Definitions   145
Appendix C: An Overview of the Personalities   155
Appendix D: Comparison Chart of Different Personality Systems   161

The Author   163

This book is written in honor of my father, Fred Littauer,
whose spiritual personality was so different from mine
that it sent me on the quest to understand these differences,
resulting in the foundation of this book.

Special thanks to my dear friend, speaker and writer Betty Southard. She did the original research on the topic of spiritual personalities. As we discussed her work, we each discovered that we shared the same interest in curiosity regarding our personality and our spiritual life. Both of us knew we had a vital and active faith, yet neither of us followed the apparent path to righteousness. Together we investigated and came to the conclusions found in this book. Betty graciously allowed me to use her research.

Thank you to my online reading group who eagerly read each chapter in its roughest form, critiqued and commented, and added their stories—enriching the text and illustrating the points I was making. I appreciate each of you!

Final thanks to Pam Morgan who jumped in to help me at the end when I was feeling stressed and unsure that I would make the deadline. Pam helped me and encouraged me.

Foreword

What a delight it is for me to read Marita's book on our spiritual personalities. The reason? It's the book I always intended to write myself but I never quite got to it. When Marita was only nine years old, our family, one by one, asked the Lord Jesus to come into our lives. As we parents got into Bible studies, we began to teach our children but found our approaches were different. My husband, Fred, went into deep study, even back into the original Greek, and wrote his prayers at least a half an hour each day. I began to teach Bible studies to women before I'd read the whole Bible. My excitement over God's word was contagious, and my interpretations changed lives. I was seeing miracles for the first time in my life.

Along with Bible studies, Fred and I began an introspective examination of the four basic personalities. Fred was an obvious Melancholy, loving serious study, and I was Sanguine, wanting to make the Bible fun. No wonder we each thought the other one wasn't "doing it right." As these eye-opening truths changed our attitudes, we began to talk to our children about their differences. When we taught Bible studies in our home, Marita and Lauren sat in. They learned about their own strengths and weaknesses at very young ages and have used this information in their personal relationships ever since.

What Marita has done in this book is show us all how to find and understand our basic personalities and then how to see the connection between personality and our method of Bible study and our relationship with God. Not only will you learn why you are different from other people, but you will also find your spiritual gifts.

While this may sound difficult at first, you will soon happily be caught up in Marita's light touch on serious subjects. This information will free you to be the best of what God intended you to be and lift any guilt you have from being the perfect Christian others expect you to be. You will learn

- Your own personality strengths
- Your individual pattern of spiritual growth
- Your God-given spiritual gifts

You will gain a whole new understanding of yourself and others and have fun doing it.

Florence Littauer
Speaker
Author of *Personality Plus* and *Silver Boxes*
Founder, The CLASSeminar
Marita's mother

Part One

What Is My Spiritual Personality?

Chapter One

The Spiritual Life of a "Good" Christian

As the pace of lifestyles quickens, the demand for
tips on how to fit prayer into a busy life grows. A
cottage industry of new books, Websites, and
spiritual aids offers quick and easy devotions.
—*Susan Hogan-Albach, quoted in* Religion Watch,
June 2001, p. 3

Each week, all over America—and much of the rest of the world—people are looking for spiritual nourishment. They go to big churches and little churches. They attend on Saturday, or maybe Sunday. Many read books, some listen to the radio, others watch religious programming on television. A few do all of the above, and others do none.

Who is right? Who is wrong?

For many years, I was sure I was wrong. I did not do any of the things that people say you are supposed to do. I heard it from the pulpit, I heard it from speakers, I heard it from friends, and I even heard it from my father: there are set things one must do to be a "good" Christian.

The two biggies are to read your Bible through (cover-to-cover in a year), and to spend an hour a day, preferably in the morning, in "quiet time" or "devotions"—even better yet, in written prayer. I know people who do this. I have one friend who is celebrating her fortieth year of reading the Bible through each year and is inviting people to join her in an online discussion as she reads through it. Wow! That surely sounds spiritual.

For the last ten or fifteen years of his life, my father embraced the idea of writing out your prayers. He hardly ever missed a day. After he died, we found notebook after notebook of his prayers. In more recent years, he used a computer. He traveled all over the country with a small laptop used exclusively for his prayers. What a great heritage I have, right? No wonder—right?—that I am writing a book on strengthening your relationship with God. Wrong.

Yes, my friend who reads through the Bible every year and my father with his diligent written prayers are both wonderful examples of godly people. They inspire me. Over and over I've made a commitment that I am going to follow their lead ("This is the year I am really going to make it from Genesis all the way to Revelation"). I bought the Bibles that divided the Scriptures into 365 daily reading segments. I bought special notebooks to help me in my written prayers. I promised God I was not going to leave the house each day until I completed the prescribed program.

I had great intentions, but I failed. Not only had I not done these things, I was consumed with guilt over my lack of discipline. I felt like a second-class citizen of the Christian world. Yet I was also sure that I had an active and vital spiritual life. I pray to God—in my head, not on paper—and my prayers get answered. I feel God's definite guidance and direction for my life, but I do not read the Bible every day.

Edy felt much the same way. She told me that the church she attends is one where they "seem to do everything right." To fit into their "Bible time" she has bought many Bibles, just hoping "this one" would make it easier for her to understand—but, Edy reported, she still couldn't get it. She tried so hard to remember Scriptures but would find the next day that she had forgotten them. She even tried sitting in her room, blocking out the world and reading. But her mind kept drifting to the things she needed tomorrow, or the laundry, or something else. Her response was to avoid talking about the Bible because she didn't feel she had a right to discuss something she knew so little about. Although Edy's Bible reading was not successful for her, she still felt sure that God was always there with her and for her. Edy told me: "I have always prayed to God and He has kept me under His wing through my very difficult life and many times of despair. I could always feel God in my heart and I just knew I had a special relationship with Him—but I did not seem to fit in."

Is it possible that there is no one right way to develop one's spiritual life?

As I speak to various groups around the country on this topic, including virtually every denomination, I find many people have tried the prescribed plans and failed. Not only do they not feel closer to God; they actually feel farther away. After hearing testimony after testimony of how a specific devotional system has been effective for others, those of us for whom these systems do not seem to work feel that the failure is not the system, but a personal deficiency on our part. This is not to say that these tried and true systems are wrong; they are just not right for everyone. What I hope to do in this book is help each person understand his or her own spiritual personality, and to develop the tools and techniques that *do* work for each of us.

If you are not already aware of your basic personality or my teaching on the general subject, you will find that Chapter Three gives you a good overview of the concepts and how they relate to your spiritual personality. Additionally, you will find a complete Personality Profile in the Appendix. If you have never taken this profile, please take some time to look at your own strengths and weaknesses before you read Chapter Three. When you take the Personality Profile, I encourage you to use the word definitions provided; they will help you select the correct words as they are intended in this usage.

One day, my friend, speaker and author Betty Southard, and I discussed the differences in personalities and how they affect one's spiritual growth and approach to God. We found that we both had the same basic experiences with the methods of spiritual growth that are touted as imperative today. Yet we each had a vital relationship with God. Until our conversation, we had felt ashamed, afraid to mention this to others.

Both of us were steeped in the teaching of personality types, and on the basis of our knowledge we developed the hypothesis that our personalities shaped our spiritual lives. Our ideas were just a theory; we needed to find out if our assumptions would prove to be true. So for more than a year, every time either of us spoke we surveyed the audiences. We posted a survey on my Website and began to gather information. The responses of more than five hundred people told us we were more right than we originally allowed ourselves to believe. Much of this book is founded on that research. You will learn from many of the survey responses as you read on.

From our questions, one respondent, Amy, told us that she had a close relationship with God from the time she was just a little girl. Having been taught "God loves you; God loves you; God loves you," Amy felt comfortable talking to Him even as a young girl. She believed God was with her on the playground, joining her on the swing.

However, Amy shared, when she was thirty-one she realized that although she never questioned God, she had never really invited Jesus into her heart as her Lord and Savior. She took that step and for a year was on her own in her quest to deepen her relationship with God. Then she joined a Bible study group, where she was exposed to the Word in a whole new way. It was a small group of well-meaning women who loved God and were committed to teaching Amy how to be His disciple. Of that time, she says, "I was in love with God and wanted so much to please Him. I lapped up their teaching like a hungry kitten at a bowl of milk."

That was a wonderful time of spiritual nourishment in Amy's life. Yet three years later she found things had changed—and not for the better. In her journal she poured out her heart to God. She told Him how she missed the times of "sitting at your feet and laying my head on your lap." She remembered how she used cry to Him because she hurt. She felt as though He put His warm, strong hands on her head and stroked her hair while allowing her to cry. He never told her to stop her tears; He was never too busy. It was in these times that Amy felt closest to God, feeling He cared for her and deeply loved her.

As Amy looked back over her journal pages, she saw she had written to God: "Do you remember even further back, when I was the skinniest kid in town—a tomboy with pigtails and scabbed knees? Remember how I'd stop right in the middle of the playground and ask you a question? Sometimes I'd wait for an answer, and sometimes not. But I always knew you were there. I never even considered you might not be. I just knew you were always delighted in who I was."

Amy shared with us that back then it was easy to connect with God. She didn't picture Him in a "throne room," as she was later taught. She never imagined she would have to get herself ready to talk to Him, never knew there was a proper way to approach Him. In her journal, she wrote: "You were just my 'Daddy,' my 'Abba.' I could curl up on your lap whenever I wanted to. I didn't realize then that I should never start my day without talking to you first. I hadn't heard that I should never cry to you because that would be 'murmuring and complaining.' You see, I never understood that there were certain rules involved in speaking to you."

Because Amy felt such a love for God, she wanted to learn all she could. She listened intently to those who taught the supposed rules. She learned the procedures, and learned them well. She even began to pass on her newfound knowledge to others, instructing them that "This is what you need to do—try this; begin this way."

Our survey made Amy go back to her journal to review her growth process. She shared another passage with us:

> But do you know what Father? I miss you! I want to put my head on your lap again and feel your hug. Yes, I know you're seated on a beautiful throne, but couldn't I just burst into that throne room when I want to share something exciting? All those rules have filled my head with so much knowledge and made me proud. Now I can impress people with how well I know the rulebook. But I don't want

that, I want you Father. I want you! I just want to be your daughter
again. I love you Abba!

Does that make you cry? Or if you are not the emotional type, does
it at least make you feel sad? It does me. It grieves me. If this fills
you with sorrow, then this book is for you! Throughout these pages
you will find many ways to strengthen your relationship with
God—ways that work for you.

As you were reading Amy's journal entry, if you said "Yes, yes;
she needs to know those rules" then this book is for you. You need
to hear the stories of others who love the Lord as much as you do
but express it in ways different from yours and different from each
other. I encourage you to expand your horizons, to allow these differences to bring unity to the church, not division.

There are some who might think what I am suggesting is hereti-
cal. Chances are they will not even get this far into these pages. But
I hope that on whichever side of the fence you sit, you will open
your heart and embrace my goal: to help my readers strengthen their
relationship with God, to have a real and vital relationship with our
God, who is alive and authentic.

So, this book is about your relationship with God. It is also about
understanding and accepting others—especially your loved ones.

My husband and I both love God, but our spiritual personalities differ considerably. We attend a megachurch. The preaching is
wonderful (hence the "mega" church status), but I'd prefer to go to
a smaller church, one where someone notices if I am there or not,
someone who misses me and gushes with enthusiasm upon my
return. When I mentioned this to my husband, he was surprised.
The anonymous quality about the church—that I dislike—is one
of the main things he likes. He can slip in unnoticed, be taught
God's Word, and leave without ever having to talk to anyone.

Jan and her husband were in a similar situation. For them church
became a point of contention. She says that "we approached our spiritual life so differently, we kept annoying each other." In hopes of
making their church attendance harmonious, Jan kept promising

herself that she would just stand there beside her husband and quietly worship God. It never worked. During the worship time, Jan is quite animated—sometimes joining others at the front to dance and sing. When she returns to her seat (at the back of the church) her husband gives her "one of those looks." He and their children silently commiserate with each other about how happy they are that they are not out of control—or making fools of themselves. When there is an altar call, Jan is out of her seat and down at the front. Jan's husband never responds because he "doesn't want to be pawed by the people who pray for you."

Jan reports: "I used to get irritated with my family because I thought they were missing out on all the blessings. My husband's approach has always been practical, private, and sedate in comparison to mine. I have always emoted, been vocal, and very exuberant."

These differences manifest themselves in church attendance and expression of worship. But they also affect those on the other side of the pew, those in ministry. Teresa is an example. Her husband is a pastor, and they work together in ministry. Yet the understanding she gained from the teaching in this book gave her fresh insights that maybe she "is not so bad."

She shared her story with me. "I have been a pastor's wife for nearly thirty years. In the early years, my husband pastored small churches, and he and I were the only 'staff' that existed. We worked together on many projects, from leading youth groups to summer trips."

She is an organizer, and coordinating an event—though challenging—can be a joy to her. As an organizer, Teresa likes to plan ahead and have her ducks in a row. She and her husband would become frustrated with each other because he thought her deadlines were unreasonable—wanting things done days before they needed to be. Likewise, Teresa felt as though she were giving freely of her time and energy, but he would wait until the last minute and then expect her to do a good job with something. It became clear that their marriage relationship would be better if they didn't try to lead church ministries together, and so they didn't—for many years.

Only after the couple learned of and understood "the personalities" that I've written and taught about for years did they grasp how their skills can complement each other. Today, Teresa says, "I'm happy to say we are very much partners in ministry and lead many ministries together in the life of our church."

Fortunately, Teresa and her husband learned about their differences and how they have an impact on spiritual life and overall ministry. Unfortunately, another respondent, Renee, did not have the same results. She was on a ministry team with a pastor who did not acknowledge and accept that one's spiritual life can take on many sizes and shapes. She was almost forty when she moved to a new city and church. She and the pastor had been friends for a year, even before she moved. So when she moved to be near that church, it was logical for her to take on leadership roles almost immediately. However, after only a few months Renee received a note with some "suggestions" of things she should do as part of her leadership/mentoring development. Her first thought was, *No problem, I can do this.*

Renee grew up with a Pentecostal/Charismatic background, played on church praise teams for years, and considers herself to be outgoing, friendly, and helpful—though she prefers to be relatively quiet with some forms of expression (hand clapping and raising hands occasionally) in her worship style. But, when she reviewed the list of "suggested" changes, she quickly saw some of the items were way outside of her spiritual personality. *I'll give it a try,* she again thought. After all, she was in a new church, experiencing new things, and the list did have some validity. So she went about attempting to incorporate each item into her worship.

The list included "Just go with the flow; loosen up; suspend all judgments and your perfectionist tendency and just enjoy worship—abandon yourself, to be a fool for Him because of His great love for you and your love for Him; laugh more and just enjoy life; when we ask all to lift hands—lift your hands; be transparent—don't be afraid of rejection; be more interactive with the group and quick to reach out to new people; be willing to get out of your comfort zone at all levels, at all dimensions."

Renee did try to grow beyond her natural tendencies. But no matter how hard she tried, she just could not work up that much consistent enthusiasm (or phony joy). As she told me the story, she said, "I was just about as loose as I was going to get." Before long, she began to resent being told how to worship. The struggle began. As part of the church's leadership program, she had to attend the services—the entire service, no slipping in after the worship—but she soon found herself wanting to completely avoid the worship service. She went, but she didn't enjoy it. It was as if she were saying, "I may be standing up on the outside, but I'm sitting down on the inside."

At the time Renee received the list, she had a limited knowledge of the personalities. Four years later, she has studied up on the subject. She wonders how the list might have been different if written with her spiritual personality type in mind. The intent of the pastor was to be helpful and cause her to stretch, but the outcome was completely the opposite. There was a period of time when she "shut down" during public, corporate worship. She said, "I can't help but think, 'If only the pastor had taken into consideration my spiritual personality and had written the list accordingly.' I have tried to learn from this experience, and I keep the list tucked away in my Bible as a reminder of what not to do to others."

Today Renee is once again able to enter into worship the way God created her—no more mask or attempts to be something she's not. She sums it up by saying, "I'm finding freedom, joy, and pleasure in His presence—like I've never known before."

Renee's story beautifully expresses the heart and soul of this book. There are many ways to show our love for God, to serve Him and to grow in Him. Our personality influences which way is the best for us. Once we understand this, we can maximize the tools and techniques that work for us and give freedom to others—who may differ from us. As I teach this material, I find the frequent conception that there is only one way, and everyone needs to do just that one thing—though as a result some people (including me) feel we must be lesser Christians because that doesn't work for us. I hope this book gives you a sense of relief and freedom while encouraging you to continue to develop your own spiritual life.

Renee's experience is especially interesting in that it is so opposite from most of the stories I hear. Usually those of us who are more expressive are being told to tone down. In her case, she was told to loosen up. It goes both ways. Whichever way we think is right is typically—without this understanding—what we think others should do as well.

How could we have such divergent spiritual needs? Could it be that God made us different for a reason?

Van has moved a lot during her lifetime. In each city, she has attended church. But she has never found one that was perfect for her. She told me:

> I used to get frustrated with the people, the pastor, the choir director, the director of women's ministries, the custodian, the yards keeper, the kitchen committee. . . . I just couldn't understand why they did things the way they did. If I happened to be in a meeting with the custodian, I focused on the flaws in the décor—not in how hard he was working, overtime, to keep up with the needs of the growing congregation. When it came to meeting with the choir director, I had my own ideas of elaborate dramas. I tended to get carried away with intricate props and costuming. It wasn't easy for me to just be the speaker at the women's banquet. I wanted a say in the centerpieces and the special music. One time I was asked to lead a workshop on teaching Sunday school. I emphasized well-presented bulletin boards, music, drama, and crafts.

Perhaps you know someone like Van in your church. She means well, but she irritates everyone—when she thinks they are irritating her! Because Van's heart was right, just trying to be helpful, she began to see that her efforts were not always appreciated. Through the principles in this book, Van began to change, to grow, and to mature.

She continues:

> Then I began to understand the differences in personality extended to our spiritual life as well. It was a harsh reality when I realized not everyone's style is to go forth with passion, color, emotion, and wild enthusiasm. I began to look around and see others were working in the church and doing a fine job—even though it wasn't my way. Others were organized, where I was not. Others were listening where I was loud. Others were caring, while I was frazzled. Stepping back, I took a look at myself. I made a personality check. There were many things I was doing well. I realized, though, that I needed to pray to God about bringing balance into my personality. Today, I operate differently than I did a decade ago. I do not rush in to fix the lilies at the foot of the cross on Easter Sunday. I do not step into others' Sunday school classes to rearrange the furniture. When the pastor speaks of the reality of life and its unavoidable hard places, I pray for those who are suffering. And, now, when someone does something that irritates me, I pray that I may not be an irritant in someone else's life that day.

As you can see, there are differences, not just in our personality but in our spiritual personality as well. In this book, we explore these differences. First, you will gain an understanding of your personality; then you'll learn how your personality has an impact on your spiritual life and your relationship with God. Second, you'll discover how you can maximize your personality to strengthen your relationship with God. Then we look at the personality of Jesus and how we can each bring balance into our personality—as Van did— by becoming more Christlike. Additionally, we do a short study on spiritual gifts and how combining our personality and our spiritual gifts equips us for the work of the church.

But now let's take a fun look at these differences as found in the fictional Sonshine Church. It might sound just like your church— maybe even too much so.

Chapter Two

The Sonshine Church

The church for people who don't do church.
—*Victory World Church billboard in Atlanta*

Sally was new in town and didn't know too many people. Having heard that going to church was a great way to make friends, she began searching for a church with people like herself. One day, on the way to the post office, she saw a sign for a new church meeting at the local high school. The sign was bright yellow and had contemporary graphic figures—like stick figures, only hip—reaching for something. She decided she would visit Sonshine Church.

When Sunday arrived, she dressed in bright, casual clothing and headed for the high school auditorium. Since the church was new, the group was fairly small, and everyone was very friendly. There didn't seem to be any of the little cliques she remembered from other churches she'd visited. The service began informally with congregational singing. The song leader wore a polo shirt, and his music selections were unencumbered by tradition. He led the enthusiastic group in fast-paced, upbeat choruses, displayed on the wall with the latest technology. The people moved to the beat and clapped their hands. After a few songs, they had a brief get-acquainted time, and everyone headed to the back of the auditorium, where coffee and donuts were served. As the music started up again, people took their coffee and headed back to their seats.

A young pastor in shirtsleeves stood up to preach. It was a short sermon with lots of emphasis on the joy of Jesus and the Christian life. He was a great storyteller, and several times people laughed out loud. This church was different from any other Sally had visited. After the service, everyone invited her to join them for lunch at a local restaurant.

That first Sunday at Sonshine Church, Sally knew she had found a new church home and became a regular attendee.

Before long, she was in charge of the birthday committee and was holding midweek meetings in her home. She cleaned her house, baked cookies, and prepared for each meeting as she would a party with friends. The group praised her for her hospitality and seemed to love her unconditionally. Within this nurturing environment, she discovered she needed to know God as these people did.

One Sunday, she went forward and prayed with the pastor. She grew spiritually week by week. Her face glowed with the love and joy of Jesus. People at her workplace noticed a difference in her, and some of them even joined her on Sundays at Sonshine Church.

A few weeks later, she noticed someone new at church who didn't seem to fit in with the group. She wore a navy blue dress with pearls, matching pantyhose, and heels. Her hair was coiffed and her face devoid of makeup. Being the friendly type, Sally made an effort to greet her. Marianne was older than most of the people who met regularly. Sally soon discovered that Marianne was the mother of Chuck, one of the young married men in the congregation. Marianne's husband had died recently, and she had moved from the Midwest to live with Chuck and his wife, Candi. She would be able to help with their children. She confided to Sally that, since she was obviously older than the rest, she thought God had brought her to this church to be a "Titus 2 woman." Not wanting to seem uninformed, Sally acted pleased with this news, went to her seat, and looked up Titus 2—at least she knew it was a book of the Bible!

Marianne's first impressions of the Sonshine Church were a disappointment. She felt unsettled in the simple church her son and his family attended. But she was glad to see they were active somewhere. She thought perhaps God also had led her there to organize her grandchildren's daily devotions, using proper children's literature. She would take them to special programs, such as vacation Bible school, held at "real" churches (the traditional ones, with a steeple and stained glass windows). Feeling overwhelmed, she cried out to God: "O Lord, I will have my hands full here. There is so much to do at Sonshine Church: so many people who need real teaching and discipline. I could start a study for young women like Sally."

Marianne spent hours at the local Christian bookstore, researching tools her flock would need in their search for spirituality. She lost herself in the commentaries and reference books and was almost late getting home before the children returned from school.

Marge worked in the reference section at the bookstore and always looked forward to Marianne's visits. These days, not too many people came in searching for deeper truths. After twenty years at the Deeper Life Bible Bookstore, Marge knew the inventory well and loved to share her knowledge with anyone who would listen. With Marge's help, Marianne soon had a resource list to recommend to the young women at Sonshine. Marianne and Marge became fast friends. Marge attended the large, traditional brick church downtown, and she invited Marianne to attend organ concerts held there on Saturday nights. Marianne purchased CDs of the organ music to play during her personal study time. The saintly sounds helped her feel closer to God.

With her mission clearly defined, Marianne started a Bible study on Tuesday evenings for young working women. First, she encouraged them to begin a daily Bible reading program with a scheduled quiet time. After all, how could she lead a Bible study with people who didn't even know their way around the Bible? The group met at Sally's house, since she already had it set up for the Wednesday night meeting. Sally loved to have her house filled with people. Besides, all the cars out front would impress the neighbors with her popularity!

Chuck had met the pastor of Sonshine Church at a business networking meeting. He sensed that the pastor viewed the church like a business; he didn't talk like the King James Bible, and he had a mission statement. Chuck liked the fact that since the church was new there were not a lot of meetings to attend. He was a busy man who did not have time for meetings—or the guilt imposed on him over not attending them. Once Chuck became a regular church attendee, the pastor put him on the board. Chuck owned his own business and dressed well, showing up every Sunday with a different power tie. He would be an asset to the church. Chuck appreciated the fact that the pastor showed discernment; after all, he had spotted Chuck's leadership skills almost the first day they met. The pastor had primed Chuck and given him a position of power.

Chuck arrived early every Sunday to set up chairs and hook up the sound system. His mother had taught him, at an early age, good organizational skills. Chuck oversaw the offering and made the bank deposits. Everyone looked up to him. His business was booming, which allowed him to build an addition onto his house for his mother, and he was sure God was blessing him because of his good church attendance.

One Sunday, the pastor preached on the power of God's presence in the Christian life. He addressed the fact that with this power a Christian could have more positive impact in his or her home and community. Chuck liked the concept of power and influence in the community; the pastor's sermon related to him. He also came to realize that what he needed most was to have Jesus in his life. He needed to talk with the pastor. Later that week, he and the pastor met, and Chuck invited Jesus into his heart and life.

Now Chuck looked forward to Sunday services with even greater zeal. The sermons made sense to him, and with the power of the Holy Spirit in his life he felt even more confident.

Fran began attending the Sonshine church for totally different reasons. She was a born follower. She was happy when Sally joined their team at work. She brightened up the office and, becoming a good friend to Fran, she brightened her life too. Sally was always cheerful and kept everyone laughing. But one day Fran noticed that Sally seemed to have an extra glow about her. Sure that it must be a new cosmetic or something, Fran asked Sally if she had changed her makeup. Sally shook her head; she was still using the same drugstore brand she'd always used. Puzzled, Fran asked, "Is anything else different?"

"I've met Jesus!" Sally gushed. "Come to church with me!" Sally's energy and enthusiasm put Fran off. She couldn't be bothered with religion and considered her Sundays an important time to catch up on sleep and reading.

Though she appeared disinterested, Fran watched Sally. She saw her pray before lunch, and she heard that others in the office had joined Sonshine Church after attending with Sally. As more of the office staff claimed to be "Christians," Fran felt that the atmosphere at work was more peaceful. There was a friendlier tone, too, which created less stress. Slowly, Fran grew interested. She asked Sally about services. Before Fran could change her mind, Sally had everything arranged. She would pick her up Sunday morning. "Don't dress up; this is a casual church," Sally said. "I'll take you out to lunch with everyone afterward—my treat!" Sally made it sound too good to refuse.

At Sonshine Church, people seemed pleased to see Fran. They didn't make any demands of her but warmly welcomed her into the group. She liked the coffee and donuts in the middle of the service too. She went back—Sunday after Sunday. Sally noticed Fran didn't have a Bible, so she went to the Deeper Life Bible Bookstore. Marge thought Sally should buy Fran a burgundy leather volume with cross-references and study notes, and a cover that held a notepad, pen, and highlighter. To Marge's disappointment, Sally instead bought a paperback modern English paraphrase with pictures.

Fran was touched by Sally's thoughtful gesture, and she faithfully carried her new Bible to church each Sunday. She was amazed that she could understand what she read and even found that sometimes she read her Bible on her own—not just in church.

One Sunday, the pastor preached on John 14:27: "I am leaving you with a gift—peace of mind and heart! And the peace I give isn't fragile like the peace the world gives. So don't be troubled or afraid" (TLB). His words touched her heart, and she underlined them in her Bible. She liked the idea of a gift; it reminded her of Sally's gift. Peace of mind and heart, and the possibility of not being troubled or afraid, were intriguing to her. At the end of the sermon, the pastor asked people to come forward to invite Christ into their life. Fran didn't move. The thought of being seen in front of everyone frightened her. She hung back and, once almost everyone had left, lightly touched the pastor's arm and whispered that she wanted to invite Jesus into her life. Standing nearby, Sally was elated. She skipped the ritual lunch party and stayed with Fran while she prayed with the pastor.

From that day on, Fran found daily comfort in the words of the Psalms. Marianne taught her to rewrite them in a journal, using her own name. This brought her great comfort and a feeling of belonging. She frequently used her Saturdays to drive into the hills with praise music playing on the car stereo. She found a favorite spot overlooking a creek. She would sit for hours on a rock, reading the Bible Sally had given her, and meditating on God's Word, the beauty of nature, and her new life. She often fell into a comfortable sleep, smiling as she rested—knowing that God loved her.

Fran shared with Sally how she was growing. She suggested that Sally try the same techniques. Though Sally was happy for her friend, the thought of sitting on a rock for hours was unthinkable to her. She preferred to spend her Saturdays shopping and listening to recorded teachings between stops. At home, she listened to the contemporary Christian music station, singing along at top volume. She also liked keeping up with news of the artists' lives. Not gifted vocally, Sally felt close to God hearing music with a strong beat and words that related to her life.

Marianne was concerned that Chuck and Candi didn't seem to have a regularly scheduled devotional or study time. How could they expect to raise their children for the Lord if they didn't set a godly example of reading God's Word every day? One night, she brought up her concerns to Chuck and Candi. At her home church, everyone was on the same daily reading program, and all used the same version of the Bible. Marianne thought that since Chuck was on the board at Sonshine, he should practice this himself and then institute the changes for everyone in the church.

Her suggestions were not well received. With their business going so well, Chuck and Candi were both working hard. They were grateful that Marianne could help with the children, but their time with them was minimal and certainly didn't allow an hour a day for devotions. Between sales calls, Chuck prayed in his car. Sometimes he listened to teaching tapes, from which he gained insights into the Christian life. Candi kept the office radio on a Christian teaching station and enjoyed the snippets she could grasp between projects. The couple often shared with each other what they were learning and debated the points on which they did not completely agree. When it was Chuck's turn to teach the midweek study, he carved out time at the office to use his Bible software and found that these were the times in which he grew the most. He had a specific goal and topic, but his schedule did not often permit such intense research. With Chuck and Candi's active and busy lives, they found that their faith carried them through, even if Marianne was concerned for their spirituality.

Sally, Marianne, Chuck, Candi, and Fran all attend Sonshine Church—as do a host of other people. Each has his or her own reasons for attending, each gets something different from the service, and each grows spiritually in his or her own way, a way suited to the individual personality.

The story illustrates how people are different. We accept that some people are outgoing optimists, and others are more introverted and serious. We know that some people enjoy people and place high priority on relationships, while others prefer to be alone, uninterrupted by others, so they can focus on the task at hand. Though we accept, and may even understand, these differences, most of us do not realize that these very idiosyncrasies that make us unique individuals also have an effect on how we view God, connect with Him, and respond to Him.

Just as the people in the fictional Sonshine Church have their own distinct spiritual personality, so do you! Go on to the next page to begin learning about yours.

Chapter Three

What Is My Spiritual Personality?

The significant mistake of the traditionalists is they require the people to start where the church is instead of the church starting where the people are. Innovators begin by asking, "What do we need to do to reach the people where they are?"

—*Leith Anderson, quoted in* Ministry Toolbox,
April 9, 2001

I have been teaching on the topic of the personalities for more than twenty years. When I address a group on the topic, I always start my basic presentation by asking two questions: How many of you have noticed that there are people out there who are different from you? How many of you live or work with—or used to live with—someone who is different from you?

The response is universal. Virtually everyone in the audience raises a hand. They know there are people out there who differ from them. This is not a new concept.

Although each person is different, there are many similarities that allow people to be grouped in general categories. The study of these differences and their interrelationship is known today as "the personalities."

Each of us has a basic personality type. It is something that comes prepackaged within our genetic makeup. Modern science has spent countless hours and dollars trying to understand where our personality comes from. We are just now beginning to get a grasp on what any teacher or parent of several children will tell you: each child comes with his or her own identity. Recent research indicates that a person's personality is determined before birth, something in the individual genetic makeup. Environment plays a role in how that personality is shaped, but the basics are predetermined.

I once had the opportunity to speak to a group of preschool directors. In doing my own little research project, I asked them if they often had siblings go through their schools. Of course, the answer was yes. I asked about these children. They had the same parents, grew up in the same house, and went to the same church and the same preschool. Often they wore the same clothes and slept in the same room. But were they the same children? No! Despite having virtually the same environment as the sibling, each child had a distinct personality. Some were incessant talkers who liked to be the focal point and whom others wanted to emulate. Others were the born leaders, telling the other little children what to do and when to do it. These children would take over the class if the teacher would let them. Others were more quiet and reserved, afraid to get messy, and avoided projects such as finger painting in favor of tidy, methodical activities like building blocks or reading. Other quiet children were content with any activity and easily went along with the program, rarely initiating any ideas of their own. These same patterns follow us throughout our lives; they are inborn personality traits.

In the Beginning . . .

More than two thousand years ago, in about 400 B.C., during the golden age of the great Greek thinkers, learned men sat and philosophized about much of life. Like today, one of the areas that aroused their curiosity was the differing nature of people. Just like the preschool teachers, they noticed that people are different. Without the benefit of contemporary science, Hippocrates, the father of modern medicine, theorized that what made people so different are the chemicals in their bodies. (Only recently have we come to see that he might have been right on more counts than we historically gave him credit for.) These thinkers believed that people could be cate-gorized into four basic groupings, and that these chemicals—or "fluids"—in their bodies are what give them the specific outward manifestations identifying their personality. The original terms they used sound foreign to our ears today because they are—they are Greek! The Greek words are Sanguine, Choleric, Melancholy, and Phlegmatic.

The Sanguine person is the high-energy, fun-loving, outgoing personality. These are the people with the bumper stickers asking, "Are we having fun yet?" Hippocrates believed these people behave this way because they have red-hot blood coursing through their veins. If you have any background in medicine, you know that the word *sanguine* relates to blood. In modern journalism, the word is used synonymously with optimism. Because *sanguine* is for-eign to most of us, I have chosen to add a modern-day adjective to it when using Sanguine to represent a personality type. Through-out this book, you will see Sanguine coupled with the word *popu-lar*, as in "she is a Popular Sanguine." If you are familiar with this teaching from another source and are accustomed to just the word Sanguine, feel free to use it. Likewise, if you have trouble pro-nouncing the Greek word or can't remember it, simply using the word Popular is fine. These ideas are not about labels; they are de-signed to help us understand ourselves and improve our relation-ship with God—and others.

The Choleric person is the one who is naturally goal-oriented, lives to achieve, and organizes quickly in her head. She (or he) is task-focused, yet outgoing, like the Popular Sanguine. The motto for these people would echo the Nike advertising slogan of "Just do it." With these positive traits, they tend to be short-tempered and bossy—which, way back when, earned them the name Choleric. Hippocrates thought these people had yellow bile in their bodies that gave them these specific traits, similar to a baby with colic or a per-son with cholera. (The preferred pronunciation of Choleric is like "collar" on a shirt, not like "calorie" count.) To make it easier to remember and understand, we have added the adjective Powerful to the Greek word Choleric to represent this strong personality type: the Powerful Choleric.

The Melancholy person is quieter, deeper, and more thoughtful. These people strive for perfection in everything that is important to them. Their motto would be, "If it's worth doing, it's worth doing right!" With perfection as a goal, this person is disappointed—and even depressed—more than the other personalities. How often have you had an entirely perfect hour (let alone a day, week, month, or year)? Hippocrates believed that this person's tendency toward depression is due to the black bile in the body causing what he termed Melancholy. The word is often used in modern-day media to represent a mood of depression or negativity. To focus on the positive aspects of this personality, we have added the word Perfect to the Greek word Melancholy, creating the personality type of the Perfect Melancholy.

The fourth personality type is the Phlegmatic. I list it last because it is less easy to identify these people. The other three personalities live life in the extreme. The Popular Sanguine is extremely fun loving, extremely loud, extremely energetic; the Powerful Choleric is extremely driven, extremely focused, and extremely goal-oriented; and the Perfect Melancholy is extremely neat, extremely quiet, and extremely organized. The Peaceful Phlegmatic is the more balanced, contented person. As such, he does not feel compelled to change the world or to upset the status quo. The original conservationist, the Phlegmatic views all of life through a filter of conserving energy. His motto might be, "Why stand when you can sit, why sit when you can lie down?" To the more driven personalities, the Phlegmatic appears to be slower than the rest, which caused Hippocrates to think that they had phlegm in their bodies, thereby giving them the name Phlegmatic. Because this word is also foreign to most of us, we have added the positive adjective of Peaceful to the Greek word Phlegmatic. Throughout this book you will see this balanced, steady, and easygoing individual described as the Peaceful Phlegmatic.

Remember, these terms are meant just to give a vocabulary by which we can discuss our personalities. They are not to put anyone in a box with a specific label. All of us subconsciously already label people, albeit with different terms, when we say things such as "She talks all the time" or "He's never met a stranger." In fact, those are comments people make about the Popular Sanguine. This person is also called a "talker." Of the Powerful Choleric, people might say "He sure gets in your face" or "If you want to get something done, ask a busy person." This person would be called the "doer" or "worker." On behalf of the Perfect Melancholy, one might say "She is so together" or "He is such a perfectionist." This person could easily be called the "thinker." When referring to the Peaceful Phlegmatic we say things like "She is so sweet" or "He is such a nice guy." This person is viewed as the "watcher."

Personality Combinations

All of us have a basic personality type, but virtually none of us is 100 percent any one type. Most of us have one dominant and one secondary personality, with a smattering of traits in the other two categories, making us each a unique individual. Sometimes the two primary personality types are closer to fifty-fifty, so that it is harder to determine the dominant and the secondary. Getting it down to such specifics is not necessary, but understanding the basic personality type is helpful because this is the filter through which we view life—even our spiritual life.

In this book, you will see a version of the chart given here, or the "squares" as we call them, in several of the chapters. The top two squares are the Popular Sanguine and the Powerful Choleric. Both of these personalities share several qualities that make them a natural combination in one person: both outgoing, optimistic, and energized by people. We place them on the top of the chart because they are both "hot" personalities, and hot air rises. When you have both the Popular Sanguine and the Powerful Choleric personality in one person, you have someone who is supercharged, super wound-up, and super high-strung, someone who accomplishes a lot and has a tendency to wear other people out. This person may be frequently questioned about being hyperactive since he has difficulty sitting still. Someone who is more Popular Sanguine will be more people-oriented. Someone who is mostly Powerful Choleric will focus more on accomplishment.

The bottom two squares are the Peaceful Phlegmatic and the Perfect Melancholy. These two are on the bottom because they are the "cool" personalities. Their cooler nature often makes these people easier to be around since they are mellow and less demanding. Both of these personalities tend to be introverted (they are energized by solitude and drained by many people placing demands on them at the same time) and pessimistic (or "realistic," as my Per-

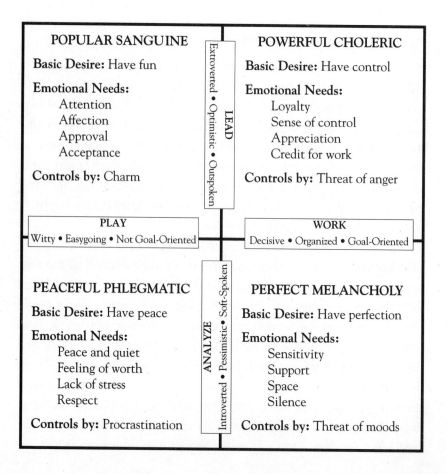

POPULAR SANGUINE

Basic Desire: Have fun

Emotional Needs:
Attention
Affection
Approval
Acceptance

Controls by: Charm

POWERFUL CHOLERIC

Basic Desire: Have control

Emotional Needs:
Loyalty
Sense of control
Appreciation
Credit for work

Controls by: Threat of anger

Extroverted • Optimistic • Outspoken
LEAD

PLAY
Witty • Easygoing • Not Goal-Oriented

WORK
Decisive • Organized • Goal-Oriented

PEACEFUL PHLEGMATIC

Basic Desire: Have peace

Emotional Needs:
Peace and quiet
Feeling of worth
Lack of stress
Respect

Controls by: Procrastination

PERFECT MELANCHOLY

Basic Desire: Have perfection

Emotional Needs:
Sensitivity
Support
Space
Silence

Controls by: Threat of moods

ANALYZE
Introverted • Pessimistic • Soft-Spoken

fect Melancholy husband says). These common factors make the Perfect Melancholy/Peaceful Phlegmatic a natural blend. This combination makes for a likeable person who also accomplishes what needs to be done. A Perfect Melancholy is more task-oriented, and the Peaceful Phlegmatic dominant is more focused on relationships.

The two squares on the right side, the Powerful Choleric and the Perfect Melancholy, are another natural combination because they are both task-oriented. This combination makes the best worker of all and is therefore the favorite of most employers. For those who have this combination and are more optimistic and people-oriented, the dominant personality is probably Powerful Choleric. Those who are more withdrawn and prefer to be alone are probably mostly the Perfect Melancholy.

The two squares on the left side are the Popular Sanguine and the Peaceful Phlegmatic. Since both of these personalities are relationship-oriented, they combine naturally. This combination is everyone's favorite person. The Popular Sanguine component makes them fun and the Peaceful Phlegmatic makes them agreeable and easygoing. As a result, their charm pulls them through most situations and makes people want to help them. As stated earlier, someone with this combination is a people person—probably primarily the Popular Sanguine. Those who are introverted are probably more Peaceful Phlegmatic.

For the purposes of this book, as we are focusing on your primary personality and less concerned with the secondary, these are the only combinations we review. However, sometimes after reading a book, hearing a speaker, or taking the Personality Profile, a person believes he or she is a combination of either the Popular Sanguine and a Perfect Melancholy or the Powerful Choleric and a Peaceful Phlegmatic. This is confusing to people because the two personality types seem to be diametrically opposed. It is true they are opposite personality types. If, after taking the Personality Profile in the Appendix, you feel one of these combinations represents you—and you want to study further—I suggest you read *Your Personality Tree.* For additional general study on this topic, you will enjoy *Personality Puzzle*, *Personality Plus*, and *Getting Along with Almost Anybody*.

Spiritual Personality

Perhaps you are already familiar with some form of teaching on this topic. Maybe you have read some of my books or heard a speaker address this topic at a business conference, or perhaps your church did a temperament study on it. Because these concepts are fairly commonplace in both the corporate and church arenas, I am presenting only a brief overview so we can move on from the same starting point. If you are familiar with similar teachings that use other names to differentiate the groupings of personality traits, don't worry. Most systems are based on the same fundamental principle, even though they use their own labels. You'll just need to translate as we go along. (A comparison chart of several systems is in the Appendix to help you translate.)

This book is not designed to be the complete tome on personality types, but rather to use the personalities as a springboard into our spiritual life: strengthening our relationship with God by maximizing our personality.

Although most of us would acknowledge that people are different, we might fail to take that understanding into all areas of life—especially spiritual life. Today's modern evangelical community, whether intentionally or not, has embraced norms that are set up on a pedestal. The expectation is that all "good Christians" follow certain standards—leaving those of us who don't do so feeling second class spiritually. Yet even the Bible presented spiritual leaders with clearly differing personalities; the terms used here are not found in the familiar versions and editions of the Bible, but examples of the distinct character traits are.

Peter

Peter is believed to have been brash and impulsive, someone who often spoke without thinking. Using the model of the personalities, we would say that he was a Popular Sanguine.

Here are three Popular Sanguine traits identified in Peter. Read the Scriptures that are noted, and draw lines connecting the Scriptures and the traits:

Matthew 26:69–75   Impulsive

Luke 24:12   Loud

Acts 2:14   Speaks without thinking

Paul

If you study the life of Paul, you will find his personality closely follows that of a Powerful Choleric. He was never afraid to face an issue head on and deal with it.

Here are four Powerful Choleric traits notable in Paul. Read the Scriptures, and draw lines connecting the Scriptures and the traits:

1 Corinthians 15:11   In your face

Acts 21:13   Hard worker

Galatians 2:11   Powerful

Acts 9:22   Uncomfortable with display
                                         of emotion

Moses

With traits that parallel the Perfect Melancholy, Moses felt a need to right wrongs and investigate details.

Here are four Perfect Melancholy traits exemplified by Moses. Read the Scriptures noted, and draw lines connecting the Scriptures and the traits.

Exodus 2:14   Uncomfortable in front of a
                                         crowd

Exodus 4:10   Fearful

Exodus 25–30   Humble

Numbers 12:3   Good with details

Abraham

Abraham is known as a man of faith; even so, his Peaceful Phlegmatic personality was still a dominant factor in his life. He had difficulty making decisions and avoided conflict. He desired security and peace.

Here are four Peaceful Phlegmatic traits Abraham had. Read the Scriptures, and draw lines connecting the Scriptures and the traits.

Genesis 12:10–20	Diplomatic
Genesis 13:7–9	Mediator
Genesis 16:3	Compromising
Genesis 18:23–33	Submissive

We can clearly see that each of these noted men of faith differed from the others. Like you and me, each had strengths and weaknesses—yet God used all of them. Each loved God, but that love, that worship, was displayed in its own way. The biblical model acknowledges differences, but where did we get the idea that how God made us might be wrong, that we have to follow a specified routine or we are not truly Christians?

This book is not a theoretical treatise to discuss the origin of the wrong ideas. Rather, I hope it will set you free from rigid thinking and allow you to strengthen your relationship with God by maximizing who He made you to be—which is shown by your personality.

The personalities are a tool that allows us to effectively develop our spiritual lives; they also help us fulfill or understand several biblical concepts.

One of my favorite Bible verses in regard to the personalities is Romans 12:18, which says, "If possible, so far as it depends on you, be at peace with all men" (NASB). I love how this verse is presented in three parts. The first part says, "If possible." It is as if God is giving us a disclaimer, as if He is saying this is something you should strive for, a goal you should try to reach. The second part says, "so far as it depends on you," making this our individual responsibility to the last part: "be at peace with all men." If this verse simply said "be at peace with all men," it would be impossible for us to do. We have all had situations with people where we have tried everything we know to do and nothing seems to work. No matter how hard we might try, we cannot be at peace with them. (I believe this is why Proverbs has all those verses about fools.) Also, no matter how hard we may try, we cannot change those other people. But as this verse suggests, we can change ourselves. We can change our approach to others so that we can, so far as it depends on us, be at peace with all men. Through the tool of the personalities, we can effectively identify the personality of others, understand their strengths and weaknesses, and adjust our approach to them.

Another passage of Scripture that is easily applied with an understanding of the personalities is Matthew 22:37–39:

> Jesus said to him, "'You shall love the LORD your God with all your heart, with all your soul, and with all your mind.' This is *the* first and great commandment. And the second *is* like it: 'You shall love your neighbor as yourself'" [NKJV].

The personalities help us with the first commandment by allowing us to break down the various aspects of God (which we address in the next chapter) and therefore truly love and appreciate all of Him. Verse 37 also says to love Him with all of *your* heart, *your* soul and *your* mind (italics mine). Depending on our individual personalities, as we see in Chapter Seven, the way my heart, soul, and mind love Him may well differ from the way yours do. For me to love Him, I need to understand me. Verse 39 tells us to love our neighbors. It doesn't say to love them if they think or act as we do. It just says to love them. Understanding personalities is an invaluable tool in learning to love our neighbors. Once we learn how our personality thrives, we can then discover how the other three flourish, and the judging stops there. Addressing how the personalities helped her apply this passage, Laurie said, "I always felt people were judging me and my unconventional ways. I felt insecure with myself. Having this new knowledge gives me the confidence I need to move and act in the way God created me."

Ruth Ann told me how the personalities helped her embrace Ephesians 2:10, which says, "For we are His workmanship, created in Christ Jesus for good works, which God prepared beforehand that we should walk in them" (NKJV). Even though Ruth Ann grew up in the church, she always wondered about this verse—until she came to understand her personality and the personalities in general. She shared, "I know that God formed me in my mother's womb and later made me a new creation in Christ. He gave me His Spirit to work in me to love others and realize His fruit in my life. But now I understand that God gave me a unique personality with certain strengths that I am to use in His service." This allows Ruth Ann, a Peaceful Phlegmatic/Popular Sanguine, to bring calm and sunshine—to a turbulent situation. She can be quiet and reflective as well as outgoing and expressive. She enjoys and benefits from solitude, but she loves the laughter of friends and the color they bring to her life. She is suited to speak up and defend the truth, give a word of encouragement, or put on an apron to serve. She explains it this way: "My personality strengths constitute the soil that the Fruit of the Spirit will grow in. And I am ordained to live my life using my personality strengths to speak the truth in love and to serve in the family of God. By doing this, I reflect my Lord."

In my life, God has used the concepts of the personalities to help me apply the idea in Ephesians 5:1–2 to my marriage. God spoke specifically to me through the version that says, "Observe how Christ loved us. His love was not cautious but extravagant. He didn't love in order to get something from us but to give everything of himself to us. Love like that" (MSG). To help me remember the concepts, I simplify it in my mind down to "Not to get, but to give." But to love my husband extravagantly, I need to understand his personality because he is so unlike me. As I understand his personality, I can give him what he needs.

I could go on. Here are a few other verses that are enhanced by an understanding of the personalities:

Each person should judge his own actions and not compare himself with others. Then he can be proud for what he himself has done [Galatians 6:4, NCV].

A man ought to examine himself. . . . [1 Corinthians 11:28, NIV]

Search me oh God and know my heart, what is way inside, the real me, try me, test me and know my way, show me how I behave and get along with others. If there be any offensive way in my actions and moods that offend or hurt other people, please help me to change [Psalm 139: 23–24, paraphrased].

I believe you can see from these examples that, even though we are unlikely to find the words Sanguine, Choleric, Melancholy, or Phlegmatic in the Bible, the concept of understanding ourselves and getting along with others is certainly a central theme in God's Word, and the personalities are a tool that allows fulfillment of those biblical mandates.

Now that you understand the basic personalities, let's look at their differences and how they affect your relationship with God—your spiritual personality.

Part Two

How Does My Spiritual Personality Affect My Spiritual Life?

Chapter Four

View of God

When we share our "picture" of God with each
other, we're expanding how all of us see God—who
is infinitely more than any of us can realize.
—*Evelyn Sloat*

Who is God? A study on the names of God offers a fascinating view
of who God is. I once did such a study and was amazed at how each
name represented a character of God. This was a new concept to
me, and it expanded my view of God. Interestingly, even though I
did this study and intellectually understand a whole picture of God,
I find that I readily—without intellectualization—embrace certain
attributes of God more than others. When I read the Bible, there
are certain types of verses I underline. Thanks to my personality
(primarily Popular Sanguine with Powerful Choleric as a strong
secondary), I find that I am attracted to those of His traits that are
like mine.

Karen's personality is much like mine. She explains, "I view
God as one who is 'fun' to be with and one who enjoys being with
me." She says she can imagine God smiling at her when she is
going off on one of her adventures—hiking in the Sierras, updat-
ing her kitchen, or camping in the desert with her grandson. She
believes He gets a kick out of her antics and says, "Go girl! I'm right
with you!" And she says, "I see God's smile of compassion and comfort when I'm in the pits over a writing rejection or a misunder-
standing with my husband or because of a rude remark from a
cranky salesperson."

Karen shares that she can also see God reflecting the Powerful Choleric side of her personality. She feels God also inspires her to stay on track, to take the lead when He nudges her to do so, and to be an example of godly commitment and integrity with everyone she encounters, from family and friends to coworkers and neighbors.

Our research shows that Karen's opinion lines up with those of other Popular Sanguines/Powerful Cholerics. God has so many characteristics that He has something for everyone. I believe Paul's comments in 1 Corinthians 9:22b are a microcosm of God: "Yes, whatever a person is like, I try to find common ground with him so that he will let me tell him about Christ and let Christ save him" (TLB). Because God has many attributes, He can find common ground with each of us.

Though all the aspects of God listed in the Bible are accurate, from our own particular personality we identify with certain parts more than others do. Let's look at each personality's perspective of God. As you read about the personality types that are not yours, you will gain insight into other aspects of God that truly are who He is. You also gain an understanding of others and the differences in their spiritual personality. Of course, there are exceptions to every rule, but our research concludes these observations are universally true.

🍃 Popular Sanguine 🍃

Those of us who have the Popular Sanguine personality view God in one of two ways—or both. The first is as the affectionate father, described in Matthew 7:11 (NLT): "If you sinful people know how to give good gifts to your children, how much more will your heavenly *Father* give good gifts to those who ask him." With that in mind, Popular Sanguines can easily understand that God would want nothing but the best for us—like a loving father.

When I was sixteen years old, I had several car accidents. Although I have always been closer to my mother—we are two peas in a pod—it was my father I called when I had the altercations. He was caring and compassionate. One of the accidents took place as I was driving to the next town over, where I was forbidden to go. Yet when I called my dad, his response was not, "Why were you on that road?" but rather, "Are you OK?" Because this is the kind of relationship I had with my father, I readily embrace the concept of God as my loving father. This is the God described in Romans 8:15 (NCV): "The Spirit we received does not make us slaves again to fear; it makes us children of God. With that Spirit we cry out, '*Father*.'"

Kathy found that seeing God as a loving father was easy for her as well. She recalls how she always felt loved by her dad. When she messed up, she was punished—and then they forgot all about it (just like God and our sins). She remembers the time her Sunday School teacher taught about David, a man after God's own heart. David sinned over and over, yet God forgave him and never stopped loving him. Kathy says, "Boy, what a relief! Next to David, I didn't look so bad. So, I knew God would forgive me and never stop loving me, just like my dad."

Upon reading the assumptions in our survey (recall Chapter One), Elaine was reminded of a pleasant memory from her childhood that shaped her view of God. She shared with me that as a Popular Sanguine she was blessed with a daddy who loved people. Growing up, she never knew she shouldn't talk to strangers. Whether her father was being a greeter to newcomers at church (long before anyone ever thought of the term or position) or talking to people in the next campsite on their summer vacations or stopping along the roadside to help the lady standing beside her stranded vehicle change a flat tire or pour water into the radiator, he was a people person. Elaine remembers that he modeled what she later learned were also characteristics of her loving Heavenly Father: peace and justice. Her earthly father took the command to care for the poor, orphaned, and widows literally. She reflects on having memories of moving out of her big bedroom on many occasions to give up her bed to a visiting missionary or a touring Bible college choir member. She told me recently, "Perhaps it is easiest for me to feel the loving embrace of my Heavenly Father when I remember the many times in church that I saw my daddy take crying, restless children (from their embarrassed parents), and walk back and forth at the rear of the auditorium until they were either quiet or asleep. Yes, I too, sometimes need to crawl into that embrace of my Heavenly Father so he can comfort me . . . and I know it's OK."

Judy is such a Popular Sanguine that she became a professional clown. In her case, she was more like her father, who was as fun loving as she is. But her dad was not around much. Her mom, a Powerful Choleric/Perfect Melancholy, was the primary influencer in her life. She remembers that although her mom was a perfect mother, she could never please her; her mom took credit for what Judy did right and blamed her for what she did wrong. When Judy came to know the Lord late in life, she thought she had to be perfect to gain God's love. Now Judy says, "But, like a loving father, God is patient, and today I feel loved by my heavenly Father."

Like Kathy, Elaine, and Judy, I was blessed by having a father who modeled God's love to me—even before he was a Christian himself. Because I had a loving father, I have no trouble embracing that aspect of God. But what about those Popular Sanguines who did not have a good relationship with their father? This is the case for Dianne. She reports, "I really try to view God as a loving and affectionate father, but since my dad was hard on us and expected a lot, I tend to think God is the same." Dianne says there are certain times, however, as she has matured in her walk with God, that she does feel He is loving and affectionate.

Like Dianne, Laurie has a difficult time seeing God as a loving father. Laurie says that she sometimes struggles with the concept of Him being ticked at her for being so lax. She often thinks of God as hard to please, just like her earthly father, despite what she knows from Scripture.

The second view of God that most Popular Sanguines hold, especially those without a good relationship with their earthly father, is as more of a best friend, someone with whom one can have fellowship. 1 Corinthians 1:9b tells us that God wants a "friend" relationship with us: "He is the one who invited you into this wonderful *friendship* with his Son, Jesus Christ our Lord" (NLT).

Dolores, a pastor's wife, found this was her situation. She says, "If you were 'emotionally estranged' from your parents, and looked to your friends, then it is easier to view God as a best friend." She states that she can relate to God as a best friend. Her dad was loving and affectionate, but nonverbal; therefore she remembers it taking a while for her to relate to God as a Father whom she could "hear."

Viewing God as a loving Father or a best friend comes naturally to those who are Popular Sanguine, but not everyone can easily accept this view. A Perfect Melancholy mom responded to our survey with this comment: "I just quizzed my resident Popular Sanguine (my son) and he said you were right with your observations about Popular Sanguines." She goes on to say that she was amazed at how readily her son gave a positive response to the question about viewing God as his best friend. This Perfect Melancholy mom confides that "I struggle trying to comprehend viewing God as my best friend, but my son views any other response as incomprehensible." This should not be a surprise because Popular Sanguines view everyone as their friend.

🌿 Perfect Melancholy 🌿

There are many places where Scripture talks about fearing God. Certainly this is an aspect of the true character of God, but Perfect Melancholies are more apt to underline these verses in their Bible (if they dare underline on the tissue-paper-thin pages).

> Thou shalt *fear* the LORD thy God; him shalt thou serve, and to him shalt thou cleave, and swear by his name [Deuteronomy 10:20, KJV].

> And remember that the heavenly Father to whom you pray has no favorites when he judges. He will judge or reward you according to

what you do. So you must live in reverent *fear* of him during your time as foreigners here on earth [1 Peter 1:17, NLT].

When surveyed about this aspect of God, one Perfect Melancholy respondent said, "My desire is to give my complete self to God continually, but sometimes I really don't know how to do that. I *fear* letting Him down, as I know I must. I *fear* that I don't understand His will for me in the way that I want to. I *fear* I am not tuned in as much as I should be, but I don't see it because of not putting in the time—but, perhaps, not putting in my whole heart!"

Viewing God as more of a Being to be revered in a *fearful* way, Debbie also perceived that she had to watch her P's and Q's: "If I didn't, He'd be sure to get me on track. That scared me."

As a Perfect Melancholy, Shelly had the same view of God. She wrote: "He is overwhelming, bigger, and greater than I can imagine. When I was young, I always pictured God as big and dark, faceless. Now I know He is loving, forgiving, and patient."

Powerful Choleric

Because control is an issue for the Powerful Choleric, and God wants to be in control of our lives, the Powerful Choleric views God as someone with whom to battle for control.

Proverbs 20:24 (NCV) addresses God's dominion over all: "The Lord decides what a person will do; no one understands what his life is all about." Philippians 4:13 (NLT) points out the need for Christ's power: "For I can do everything with the help of Christ who gives me the strength I need." Yet Powerful Cholerics keep making plans, as addressed in Proverbs 19:21 (MSG): "We humans keep brainstorming options and plans, but God's purpose prevails." Rather than trying to do it on our own, James 4:14–15 (GW) teaches what we should do: "You don't know what will happen tomorrow. What is life? You are a mist that is seen for a moment and then disappears. Instead, you should say, 'If the Lord wants us to, we will live and carry out our plans.'"

Other personalities can give God control of their lives, but this is difficult for the Powerful Choleric. At a Bible study I attend, I was given a copy of this poem, which perfectly sums up what the Powerful Choleric does with God:

Just as a child brings his broken toys with tears,
For me to mend,
I took my broken dreams to God
Because He was my friend.
But then . . . instead of leaving Him in peace to work alone,
I hung around to help
With ways that were my own.
At last I snatched them back and cried "How could you be so slow?"
What could I do my child, He said,
You never did let go.

—Faith Mitchner

That poem perfectly illustrates what Anne went through in her life as she fought with God for control. She told me she had a true opportunity to see God at work in her life when she was at the end of her rope in relationships with men. She had gone from one guy to the next, always trying to fix them and make them the man God would approve for her. Of course, it never worked, and she had a particularly horrible ending with her last boyfriend. Anne was struck with the fact that she was attracting the same kind of man over and over. She went to church and tried to draw close to God, all the while living in sin between Sundays.

It was after the last episode that Anne finally, with all her heart, threw her hands up in the air and with absolute admission of her sin and desire for God's will in her life asked God to never let another man come into her life unless he was the one God had designed for her. Anne remembers that within one month, God showed her who her husband was going to be. He was someone she had known at church for almost a year, and she wasn't even attracted to him. He was so nice and very godly. They have now been married for five years. Anne says, "It has been the best five years in my life and continues to be better and better everyday." She continues: "Today my husband is being groomed for an associate pastor position at our church. Quite a long way from the deadbeat guys I used to go after!"

Even as a child, Powerful Choleric-Perfect Melancholy Renee knew she was in control. She remembers when she was just three or four years old, swinging in the backyard, and calling out over and over again, "'Daddy . . . Daddy . . . Daddy," when to her surprise her dad suddenly appeared from around the corner of the house. All her life since then she thought it was because she wanted him to come, and called for him, that he came. It wasn't until she had gotten much older that she realized it was, in fact, time for him to come home from work. When he arrived home at that formative moment, he had heard her calling from the backyard and like any "good" dad came to her. Today the same confidence has carried into her relationship with God. Renee says, "If I call, He will come. If I have a need, He will answer."

🍃 Peaceful Phlegmatic 🍃

The Peaceful Phlegmatic is attracted to verses about God that address God as a place of comfort and rest:

> He maketh me to lie down in green pastures: he leadeth me beside the still waters [Psalms 23:2, KJV].

> May our Lord Jesus Christ and God our Father, who loved us and in his special favor gave us everlasting *comfort* and good hope, *comfort* your hearts and give you strength in every good thing you do and say [2 Thessalonians 2:17, NLT].

> Moses said this about the people of Benjamin: "The Lord's loved ones will lie down in safety, because he protects them all day long. The ones he loves *rest* with him" [Deuteronomy 33:12, NCV].

Blessed be the God and Father of our Lord Jesus Christ, the Father
of mercies and God of all *comfort*, who *comforts* us in all our tribula-
tion, that we may be able to *comfort* those who are in any trouble,
with the *comfort* with which we ourselves are *comforted* by God
[2 Corinthians 1:3–4, NKJV].

Notice variants of the word *comfort* used five times in the last passage.

I received an e-mail from Terri, acknowledging that this aspect
of God rang true for her:

> Many times I think I have to work at getting back in God's "good
> graces" or I have to prove to Him that He is #1 in my life, even if I
> didn't have "devotions" that morning like that inner tape recorder
> tells me I am supposed to do. I wanted to please God growing-up
> and I thought I was. Then my world turned upside down to the
> point that the real me started coming out. I began to realize that I
> had learned to pretend very well. The smile that was always there
> and the "cheerful" obedience to those over me were carefully placed
> in position by years of experience in pretending.

Terri's husband became a quadriplegic in 1980, and she suddenly
found herself with him and three preschoolers to take care of and
raise. Feelings she never knew existed began to come out, and they
threatened the core of her relationship with God. She says, "Years
of fearing God and pleasing Him, because I was supposed to, weren't
really enough to sustain me when it came to the nitty-gritty living
of life after the 1980 accident."

Terri realizes that these many years following the accident have
become the basis for the beginning of a transformation: in her relationship with God, her whole view of God, and understanding who
He really wanted to be to her. She says, "God went from being not
only the Sovereign God over me, controlling everything in the
world around me, but my Refuge and my Comforter, Who invites
me to pour out my broken spirit to Him."

Though Sharen's experiences were different from Terri's, she found the same comfort in God. Sharen remembers longing for peace. In her touching story, she shares that her young life was filled with argument after argument—including some physical abuse. When she was eight years old, there was a short-term reprieve: her parents divorced. Almost immediately thereafter, her mother moved Sharen and her brother to Southern California, ending her reprieve. While her mother took secretarial training classes, they lived with her grandparents. Her grandfather, who is now deceased, was a pedophile and took full advantage of the situation by sexually abusing her for six years.

Sharen reflects, "I was a very frightened and confused little girl, keeping a secret from everyone . . . except God. I was able to run to God through all my childhood years, without finding Him at fault for my circumstances. He's the One who calmed my fears, comforted my pain, and soothed me when I cried. I went toward Him as a place of refuge and rest."

I received another story that shared similar elements with Sharen's. The respondent asked to remain anonymous—which I will, of course, honor. However, before I share her story with you, I want you to know why she wants to be an unknown contributor. As someone who is not a Peaceful Phlegmatic, I found her comments to be quite insightful. She states, "I know one of the reasons Peaceful Phlegmatics are closed. We need respect but we've learned from experience that we don't get it. The Popular Sanguines will gossip, Powerful Cholerics will judge us and find us wanting, and Perfect Melancholies will criticize."

Let me share this story in the respondent's own words:

As a small child, I felt abandoned by my parents' divorce and was raised by my grandparents. At age thirty, my life fell apart when I divorced my unfaithful, abusive, alcoholic husband, only to get into a relationship with a man who beat me and attempted to murder me.

> After I emotionally staggered out of that painful relationship, I had a heart-to-heart talk with God and said, "OK, since I've already gone through this hell, You might as well make the trip worth something."

She shared that she doesn't exactly know what the balm of Gilead is, but she does now know that Jesus' love is balm to her soul. At times she feels she has gaping holes in her heart from its being violently clawed out. However, in healing her hurts Jesus has filled her heart with His compassion. From her experiences, she has come to understand compassion as giving to others the comfort Jesus has given to her.

In her work, this respondent said, "I have the opportunity to talk with people from different places and in many walks of life. Although my ministry isn't specifically targeted to the abandoned, the abused, or the self-absorbed, I make a point to have my radar out and respond with an encouraging word to the lonely person in the crowd, the frightened child, or the foolish woman who is about to destroy her home with her own hands."

She normally doesn't tell people about this part of her life, but occasionally God's Spirit prompts her to tell it to other people so they will know the veracity of the comfort of Christ.

Each of these views of God is truly a part of Who He is. He is a loving Father. He is a best friend. He is someone for whom we should have reverence or fear. He does want to be in control of our lives. He is a place of comfort and rest. Yet from our own spiritual personality, we more quickly embrace the part of God that is most like us.

Once you know your own personality and understand the aspects of God that you accept, yet know that these other elements of God are real too, you remove the confusion you may feel by trying to live under someone else's standard—like the Perfect Melancholy mother who struggles to "comprehend" her son's view of God as a best friend.

Next, we look at our worship experience and how our personality shapes the standard of the church, music, and preaching that work for us.

View of God

Loving Father or Best Friend

If you sinful people know how to give good gifts to your children, how much more will your heavenly Father give good gifts to those who ask him.
Matthew 7:11 (NLT)

He is the one who invited you into this wonderful friendship with his Son, Jesus Christ our Lord.
1 Corinthians 1:9b (NLT)

Someone to Fight for Control

We humans keep brainstorming options and plans, but God's purpose prevails.
Proverbs 19:21 (MSG)

You don't know what will happen tomorrow. What is life? You are a mist that is seen for a moment and then disappears. Instead, you should say, "If the Lord wants us to, we will live and carry out our plans."
James 4:14–15 (GN)

A Place of Comfort and Rest

May our Lord Jesus Christ and God our Father, who loved us and in his special favor gave us everlasting comfort and good hope, comfort your hearts and give you strength in every good thing you do and say.
2 Thessalonians 2:17 (NLT)

Moses said this about the people of Benjamin: "The Lord's loved ones will lie down in safety, because he protects them all day long. The ones he loves rest with him."
Deuteronomy 33:12 (NCV)

Someone to Fear

Thou shalt fear the LORD thy God; him shalt thou serve, and to him shalt thou cleave, and swear by his name.
Deuteronomy 10:20 (KJV)

He will judge or reward you according to what you do. So you must live in reverent fear of him during your time as foreigners here on earth.
1 Peter 1:17 (NLT)

Chapter Five

Worship Experience

There are many different and acceptable ways of demonstrating our love for God. Our personality will lead us to be more comfortable in some of those expressions than others, and that is perfectly acceptable to God. In fact, by worshipping God according to the way He made us, we are affirming His work as Creator.

—*Gary Thomas*, Sacred Pathways

If you have ever been church shopping, you know what a daunting task it is. If you have had to find a new church with a spouse, you know it is nearly impossible to settle on one you both like.

Why are there so many churches out there? Some have hymns and organ music, while others have a full band. I have been in churches full of people where the pastor shouts, spewing saliva across the first few rows. I went to a church once where there were banners on the walls and people took them off the walls at will and paraded up and down the aisles waving the banners in time to the music. A friend of mine attends a church that has spent a full year in the book of Galatians—going over every nuance and original-language meaning of words.

I once visited my aunt's church, where the minister's main message was that "the one true constant of the church was the church coffee hour" (a congregation for the Starbucks crowd in pre-Starbucks days). My cousin Laurie is a minister. She wears an ornate robe with a seasonally appropriate stole. I've only seen my pastor in a coat and tie once, conducting the funeral of my friend's husband. He is dressed fashionably. I often point out his clothes to my husband, suggesting that he'd look good in something like that. Within a few days, we have created a copycat outfit. We look to him for spiritual guidance as well as an enhanced fashion sense.

What I look for in a church is clearly defined, but there are all kinds of churches with preaching, music, or clothing styles that are not my choice—yet they too are filled and flourishing.

How much impact does our personality have on our total worship experience? A lot. Though not entirely the deciding factor, our personality definitely influences what type of service appeals to us. Thinking of her own spiritual journey, Van said, "Today, I realize that I am most content in a church that caters to my personality."

Let's look at how each personality's worship is typically played out.

🍃 Popular Sanguine 🍃

For the Popular Sanguine, church is often an extension of one's social life—which complements the spiritual experience. Because these people like to have fun, they prefer a preacher who has a good sense of humor and look forward to visiting their friends. As I mentioned earlier, when I go to church I expect to visit my friends. When I first moved to Albuquerque, the church is where I met most of the women who became my "buddies."

Addressing her natural church preferences, Van wrote: "As a Popular Sanguine, I am attracted to a sanctuary that is pleasing to the eye—with dramatic color and light. It needs to be nicely decorated, with a warm and inviting atmosphere. I like the service to be upbeat—definitely not monotonous—with a variety of music that is well presented by a choir that is as close to professional as you can get. I may not sing, but I am drawn into worship when I hear music that is in the right key and see a choir that looks good."

Like me, Van said she wants to hear a preacher tell stories with humor because she needs to laugh. She does not like sermons about suffering and reality. Because she is a Popular Sanguine, she wants a friendly church that includes her in things like the decorating committee. She meets new people easily, so she'd be delighted to be on the welcoming committee. Since Van loves parties, the fellowship committee calls to her sense of fun. She concluded her church review by saying, "It thrills me to be up front, leading the devotional, sharing my testimony, or giving a presentation at a banquet. My desire is to be in a church where I can help the ladies get away from the doldrums of life by planning a mountain retreat, a trip to a beach cottage, meeting for coffee or going to a local trendy restaurant where we can go to get away from it all—returning to life refreshed. I want a church that lets me get involved!"

As a Popular Sanguine/Peaceful Phlegmatic, Sharen had a tough time finding a church that fit everyone in her family. She told me about her experience after a cross-country move. She remembers being anxious to find a church for her family again. She shares, "Our children had grown up in our last church, and it was truly our family. I had been mentored by a faithful woman of God in women's ministry, and was ready to meet my new family and begin serving."

Sharen found that it was a year before they settled on one, but not without difficulty. She told me she's not so concerned about the preaching, except that it be teaching, not spewing. She loves the worship since it is a time she can gather with her "family" and lose herself in adoration of the Lord. It's easy and she doesn't care if they sit or stand, raise hands or not, but she wants the freedom to do any of it. She exclaimed, "I love it all!" And then there's the handshaking and hugging; she loves that too. If they don't do things in their proper order, Sharen doesn't care one way or the other. She just relaxes and enjoys the service. Her optimistic personality doesn't want to find fault in the service—ever. She's frustrated when someone in her family deciphers every single word and anecdote to find out what "he really meant," asking, "Are you sure that's scriptural?" Instead, Sharen asks, "What's the application for me?" She is careful to check on the soundness of the teaching, but she doesn't like conflict or arguing about the sermon: "I want *grace*! I want my family to extend *grace* and not pick things apart. I realize this is their personality to do what they do. The thing I don't understand is how they stay on the task of the conversation and not get emotionally frustrated. I feel like I just want to cover my ears."

Sharen realizes that others in her family are Peaceful Phlegmatic; they just sit quietly. She says, "I wonder if they feel like me? I worry that they're being hurt sometimes. Or maybe they're just silently daydreaming, ignoring the whole conversation. Occasionally one of us will pipe up and say, 'Stop arguing!' The Powerful Cholerics turn in disbelief and with a wave of the hand say, 'We're not arguing, it's just a conversation.'"

Sharen told me that understanding the concept of spiritual personalities opened her eyes to the reasons why she and her husband have always had difficulty settling on a church home.

With both of her children now adults, but still at home, Raelene has had to accept that they cannot find a church with which they are all happy. She and her husband have always enjoyed a traditional-contemporary style church, traditional in program but more contemporary in worship and outreach. (The traditional is for her Powerful Choleric side and the contemporary for her Popular Sanguine side. Her husband, Chip, is a Peaceful Phlegmatic, so what made her happy was usually OK with him.)

Raelene and Chip were surprised to learn that their twenty-year-old daughter, Megan, a Powerful Choleric, wants to be in a large church that is geared toward younger people. Megan wants nothing traditional, all contemporary, except that they be grounded, with their own building and lots of programs.

In contrast, Aaron, Raelene's eighteen-year-old Peaceful Phlegmatic/Perfect Melancholy son, wants to be in a small church that is creative in its music and the presentation of the Word. The flow of the service can be different every week—no canned program. There can be nothing traditional, unless it's a hymn redone to current music. The churches he likes are the kind that typically don't have their own building but rather meet in schools or strip malls.

Raelene shared with me that it's been very difficult as parents to not have their kids with them as a family at church. She said,

"We've finally learned that if we hope to have our children continually grounded and growing as Christians, we had to allow them to be in the kind of church that fits their own spiritual personalities." For Raelene and Chip, this may mean their children attend other churches, but it doesn't mean a different God, for indeed He created them to find Him and worship Him in their own unique way.

🌿 Perfect Melancholy 🌿

The Popular Sanguine prefers flash; the Perfect Melancholy is attracted to a planned and predictable service without a lot of personal involvement.

Campbell explains that this is why he is a Presbyterian: "I am comfortable with the orderly form of government. Occasionally when we visit another church, I find myself getting nervous after three praise songs have been sung. It is out of my comfort zone. I find peace in the quiet reverence of the sanctuary—it doesn't require much socializing." When they go to visit his wife's family, Campbell is always in fear that the pastor will ask him to open the service in prayer. He likes to be prepared. He explained, "I do not fit into a service where they expect you to stand up at the spur of the moment and praise God or close the service by holding hands with the stranger next to me."

Kate's taste agrees with Campbell's. As a Perfect Melancholy she feels that structure and consistency are important. When others don't participate in the same way, she tends to think they are lazy and not spiritual. Kate states that "attending church, Sunday school and Bible studies is extremely important as I sense my need to be fed on a daily basis as being crucial to my spiritual health."

Fran told me about her dad and stepmother. He is Perfect Melancholy/Peaceful Phlegmatic. She is Peaceful Phlegmatic/Perfect Melancholy. Fran shared that they have joined the Third Order of the Franciscans and now do contemplative prayer every Monday. Her dad and stepmother feel strongly that to get close to God you must spend lots of time with Him. They pray for an hour every morning, read their Bibles every day, and pray at every meal, and they have a strict schedule. Fran shares, "Dad is always trying to get me to come during these times but I enjoy the dynamic of the regular service and the contemporary music." Fran likes contemporary, while her dad prefers a quieter service.

Irene is a Perfect Melancholy who, when faced with a change in the church service, struggled with the contemporary. She told me, "When the praise and worship movement hit our very conservative church, I was extremely uncomfortable. The hand-raising, shaking of hips and handclapping really made me nervous. It looked to me like 'dancing,' and that just wasn't acceptable to my Perfect Melancholy mind. I was so distracted by watching that it began to affect my worship." Irene realized that she was becoming judgmental and critical of those people, but God helped her realize that different personalities worship as they choose. Now Irene says, "I needed to be myself and concentrate on my own style of worship, and not let the others hinder me in worshipping the same Lord and Savior."

🍂 Powerful Choleric 🍂

The Powerful Choleric is less concerned with the frills and looks more for good, practical Bible teaching—with emphasis on the practical. My friend who is in the church that is spending a year in Galatians is frustrated because understanding the Greek meanings of words is nothing she can use in her everyday life.

At my church, I think the preaching is the strong suit. As someone who is half Powerful Choleric, I appreciate the preaching but dislike the style of music, which feels as though it is droning on and on. So my husband, who is also part Powerful Choleric, and I arrive in time to catch a song or two (not a half hour of music) and hear the sermon—which is why we as Powerful Cholerics go to church in the first place.

Kate is also half Powerful Choleric. She reports, "When it comes to sermons, my Powerful Choleric takes over. I want the practical application of what is being taught—tell me what to do with it."

Speaking of sermons, Dana observed that the personality of the pastor has an impact on how the weekly message is delivered. This was never more obvious to her than over the last fifteen years. The church she and her husband attended had two copastors. One was a Popular Sanguine and the other very much a Powerful Choleric. On a given Sunday when the Popular Sanguine pastor was delivering the message, Dana, a Popular Sanguine, would leave the service encouraged and talking ninety miles an hour about what the Lord had showed her. On the Sundays when the Powerful Choleric pastor delivered the message she would leave a little overwhelmed. One Sunday, as Dana and her husband headed home, she brought this to his attention. She told her husband, "When [this pastor] preaches I only understand about the last fifteen minutes of the sermon when he applies it." Dana shared with me what happened next. She said, "My husband, a Powerful Choleric himself, shook his head and replied, 'Well, when the other pastor teaches he could say everything he has to say in fifteen minutes.'"

Louise is a Popular Sanguine, and her husband is a Perfect Melancholy. Like Dana and her husband, Louise found their personalities directly affect their taste in preaching. Louise belonged to a large church with two pastors in rural America. When one pastor—who she believed to be a Popular Sanguine—left, for almost a year the church stayed with just a Peaceful Phlegmatic pastor. Louise, a Popular Sanguine, truly felt as if the Holy Spirit were no longer sitting in pew eight (the pew where her Perfect Melancholy husband thinks they must sit). She remembered, "I never noticed how 'dull' this pastor was before, probably because the other pastor, when not preaching the sermon, had spiced up the service with his dramatic reading of scripture and adding humor to the announcements." It was at this time in her life that Louise found a television evangelist and authors to fill the void she was feeling. A new Popular Sanguine pastor was anxiously received—none too soon for her liking. She says that her Perfect Melancholy husband did not share in her joy and excitement at the new pastor; he thought things had been just fine during this period because of course the service was consistent and predictable.

We might think that younger age groups don't really care about church. Alex, a college student and a Powerful Choleric, has definite opinions. He would like to bring back the Doxology, the Lord's Prayer, and the Apostle's Creed—believing they belong in every service. Alex doesn't currently attend church anywhere because he has no control in that environment. While discussing his need for control, Alex said, "I talked to the minister of the college group. It was clear that he was a Powerful Choleric too. There is no room for two Cholerics." His mother, Van, states that she shouldn't be surprised. She remembers when they first brought Alex to church as a toddler. Throughout the entire special music, he kept repeating, "I direct it. I direct it." Later Van told me the story of when Alex finally wiggled out of his daddy's arms and ran with his arms flailing like the music director's. When his daddy caught up to him and scooped him up to return to the pew, Alex was frustrated; he wanted to direct the choir. He sobbed until they finally had to take him from the sanctuary. The following Sunday, Alex lined up all the toddlers in his Sunday school class and created his own choir.

🌿 Peaceful Phlegmatic 🌿

As you might assume, the Peaceful Phlegmatic has less defined opinions about what a church service should look like, or how their worship experience should take shape.

Ben doesn't care where he worships. He has no opinion. Any preacher is fine, as long as he is not loud. He would rather not have to stand to sing hymns or read the Word of God. He would be happy to sit through the entire service. When he heard that the disciples and Jesus were "reclining" at the last supper, he thought that custom would be a wonderful idea. But he said, "I am not so enthused about the practice that I would try to make changes to the communion service. Trying to change an entire congregation would be too much work." In addition to Ben's agreeable approach to church attendance, he wants the family to agree with the sermon, having no heated debates or differing opinions on the way home. Ben says, "Sundays are my favorite day because a nap is expected after lunch. No chores are planned and there are no expectations to be met, except, of course, to go to church."

Like Ben, Fran's husband (a Peaceful Phlegmatic/Popular Sanguine) doesn't get too involved in church. Fran wrote me saying that when they attend church they learn to use each other's strengths; he likes to just sit there and sing quietly, while she likes to raise her hands and sing loudly. Fortunately, their church does a good mix of contemporary Christian music and the old-fashioned hymns. Fran, of course, loves the contemporary stuff while her husband likes the old favorites. Fran and her husband have found what works for them: he sits quietly and listens to the preacher while she takes notes and follows along in her Bible.

Bev shared her husband's attitude about church with me. For Pat, also a Peaceful Phlegmatic, being a background person is important. He is happy to attend a church that is peaceful and orderly and where the sermon gives direction, but one that doesn't call for too much action or commitment. Being an usher suits him well, since he can greet people and show them to a seat but doesn't have to carry on an extended conversation.

Bev said once they were attending a small church with a "family" atmosphere. The teaching was scriptural and applied directly to daily life and relationships in the church and family. The members were warm and friendly. During the service they would break into small groups, sharing prayer needs. Then they would have a time of prayer, still in the small group. Anyone could pray aloud as they were led. Bev enjoyed this time of interaction and usually prayed each time. Pat was happy to be ushering nearby since it kept him from having to get involved. Bev remembers, "He would later tell me that he had heard me praying. He seemed to say it with pride; he was happy that I would pray, for it is something that he isn't comfortable doing with others."

The Peaceful Phlegmatic does tend to be more flexible, though knowing when he or she has found what is comfortable. Maxine, a Powerful Choleric, shared with me a story about when she and her Peaceful Phlegmatic husband went church shopping. They visited every church in town when they moved into their new retirement community. They knew exactly what they were looking for but couldn't seem to find it. They found churches that were filled with unfriendly people, and some were filled with mostly young people. Some played the music too loud, and some didn't have music at all.

Finally, Maxine and her husband found their new church home. She told me, "The praise and worship was wonderful, the church doctrine agreed with ours, the people were friendly, and the pastor remembered our names the second time he met us! We became members shortly after our first visit."

But after a while, Maxine realized that she had become bored. She still loved the praise and worship, but she didn't feel she was getting fed spiritually. Her husband was content, and when she listened to others at their weekly Bible study rave about the pastor's Sunday sermon, she thought, *Did they hear the same sermon I did?* She didn't think it was meaningful at all.

A year passed, and then another. Maxine began visiting other churches again, popping in at her old church for Sunday evening services or weekday services. She saw a few pastors she found inspiring and motivating and even begged her husband to attend with her. He never cared for those other services and made it clear he had no interest in changing churches. All of their friends were also happy, commenting frequently about the pastor's "wonderful Sunday message." She said, "I decided it must be me, and determined each Sunday to focus harder on what the Pastor was saying."

Maxine really did try, but her mind continued to wander as the pastor delivered his message in his usual unemotional way. She continues, "I tried to follow the sermon outline in the bulletin, but usually had the blanks filled in before he even got to them." Then one day "the personality light bulb" went on for her, and she began to understand it all better. After she dragged her husband to visit another church, he complained that he felt he was being shouted at. The pastor spoke in a loud voice that met her personality needs. As a Peaceful Phlegmatic, her husband was at peace with their pastor's teachings because the messages were general and unemotional, delivered in a soothing voice. Maxine states: "The atmosphere of the sanctuary is one of beauty and tranquillity. The lights are dim, adding to the serenity. Even the sermon outline pleases his spiritual personality. It is simple and orderly, not requiring deep analytical thought."

Maxine's Powerful Choleric personality was crying out for action. She wanted to hear messages about God's power and might. She wanted to be taught about the power of praise and of spiritual warfare. She was ready to lead the battle, and was waiting for the battle cry! Maxine states, "I like a pastor to raise his voice, to move around as he talks to people, to pound his fist if he needs to in order to get a point across."

As Maxine thought about some of the other people in their Bible study who often praised the pastor's sermons, she realized that they too had a high percentage of the Peaceful Phlegmatic personality—with one or two Popular Sanguines thrown in. She started to see how a Popular Sanguine would also be happy in the pretty setting, and with sermons that did not require the listener to work on anything. They would love the social activities of the church and seeing all their friends.

So Maxine has learned to compromise, and her husband has agreed to visit another church with her once a month. She says, "I am happy that he accompanies me, and I respect his comments, now that I understand why he feels the way he does. I enjoy the many positive aspects of our church, and look for the teachings that I need and enjoy through books and tapes, and monthly battery charges at another church. God made us all a little different, so that we can all love and serve him a little differently."

Maxine has caught the vision—and the challenge. On the basis of our spiritual personality, we are each naturally drawn to different things in our worship experience. The challenge comes when we are married to someone who seeks something different from what we like (and we are, it seems, almost always married to someone who is the opposite personality from ours). How do we find a church we both like? As Maxine and her husband have done, one usually needs to compromise. As Maxine has done, those of us who compromise need to find other ways to nourish our souls.

Ruth and her husband have also been church shopping and found that compromise is in order. She says, "Understanding that churches have their own personality, and that the pastor's person-ality will impact the church if he is there long enough, has helped us loosen up our expectations as we continue to look for a new church home. We have concluded that we may have to compro-mise by attending more than one church a month. Or we may need to choose one church home and start a parachurch ministry that will let us do some customizing where the personality of ministry is concerned."

If your church doesn't cater to your personality, remember: this is what your personal quiet time is all about. A church is made up of all kinds of personalities. We must be careful not to push too hard for what we need, and in turn to accept that others have needs too. In Chapter Seven, we look at the variety of ways in which each personality can grow closer to God.

Chapter Six

Spiritual Strength

> It's time to reject shame and embrace joy. It's time
> to begin defining who we are in relation to Christ
> and one another and reject definitions provided by
> others. It's time to control our theology and
> practice our faiths.
>
> —*John Lepper, quoted in* Baptists Today,
> *May 2000, p. 7*

If you study the Bible thoroughly, you will see many basic spiritual
themes repeated over and over again. Some of the most prevalent
are grace, knowledge, justification, and the sovereignty of God.
Each of these spiritual strengths represents a strong suit of each personality. Again, all are wonderful qualities, but depending on our
own personality we gravitate to one aspect more than the others.

☙ Popular Sanguine ☙

Because Popular Sanguines naturally feel that everyone likes them
and they are accustomed to skating through life on their charm,
they have no trouble with the idea that God loves them too. To the
Popular Sanguine, grace is a natural extension of that love.

> And if He chose them by *grace*, it is not for the things they have
> done. If they could be made God's people by what they did, God's
> gift of *grace* would not really be a gift [Romans 11:6, NCV].

> And all need to be made right with God by His *grace*, which is a free gift. They need to be made free from sin through Jesus Christ [Romans 3:24, NCV].

To grasp the affinity of the Popular Sanguine to grace, we must first have a basic understanding of what it is. I recall memorizing a definition of grace from my junior church days: "Grace is God's unmerited favor." That is a nice, short definition, but it really does not explain a lot. Looking further, I found quite a bit of controversy as to what grace really is. For the intent here, I selected this from the New Unger's Bible Dictionary:

> Grace thus rules out all human merit. It requires only faith in the Savior. Any intermixture of human merit violates grace. God's grace thus provides not only salvation but safety and preservation for the one saved, despite his imperfections. Grace perfects forever the saved one in the sight of God because of the saved one's position "in Christ." Grace bestows Christ's merit and Christ's standing; "for in Him all the fullness of Deity dwells in bodily form, and in Him you have been made complete" (Colossians 2:9–10). Grace thus obviates any obligation to gain merit, and the law as a merit system is no longer applicable to a believer, since he is no longer "under law, but under grace."

I selected this definition because it points out the elements of grace that are naturally attractive to the Popular Sanguine. In essence, we do not have to do anything to earn God's favor. Despite our "imperfections" we have "Christ's merit and Christ's standing."

You mean I don't have to do anything to get God to love me, to get His approval? Sign me up!

In Lory's life, God's grace manifested itself this way: "About failing God and guilt, perhaps we Popular Sanguines just take God and his grace at face value. We all know salvation can't be earned, it's a gift from God. So beating ourselves up over not earning something that can't be earned anyway is rather silly and a waste of time." Lory believes we should not just get on with the lives He calls us to—taking to heart what Paul says in 2 Corinthians 12:9 (NCV): "My grace is enough for you. When you are weak, my power is made perfect in you." She says, "I am very happy to brag about my weaknesses. Then Christ's power can live in me."

Linda summed it up simply by saying, "I think spiritual failure does not keep Popular Sanguines from trying again. For each day is a new, fresh day." Because we live our lives in a perpetually apologetic mode, we especially value the concept of grace.

Armené felt she was always apologizing to God for her failures. She told me, "God relieved me of my guilt one day when I was so frustrated with all my failed good intentions. I just couldn't keep the devotional schedule that I kept making for myself. It was sort of like a perpetual New Year's resolution that lasted twenty-four hours." She would commit to an early morning time, and then find a million things that needed doing in the early morning. She tried an evening time, and promptly fell asleep after about ten verses. One day, while doing the dishes, she remembers beating herself up about all of this and asking, "What was wrong with me? Didn't I care about Jesus? Was I just lazy?" She continues, "I couldn't stick with it. I probably would have fallen asleep in the garden of Gethsemane and missed the whole crucifixion! Jesus couldn't count on me." Then, in the middle of this whole self-torture session, Armené felt as though God said to her, in a voice that a father would use to distract a miserable child, "I tell you what. Let's do this . . . You go ahead and get busy with your day. But keep your ears open and listen for my voice. I will pick a time and place to meet you and when it is ready I will call you. It will be a surprise each day. When you hear me call, you meet me and we will have our special time together." She said that it was suddenly like a game. Never the same place, never the same time. In doing that, God took all the "shoulds" out of her meeting with him, and instead of "having devotions" she had intimacy and developed a sharpened ear that got used to listening for His voice. She shares the result: "This helped me to learn that God accepted me just as I am and taught me that I can count

on Him to even design the disciplines of spiritual growth around
who He had made me to be. He is so good!"

That in a nutshell is grace—and Popular Sanguines need a lot
of it.

🍃 Perfect Melancholy 🍃

The spiritual strength that attracts the Perfect Melancholy is
knowledge. Perfect Melancholies like details, facts, charts, and lists.
This inherent personality trait carries into their Christian life as
well. Popular Sanguines are happy coasting through life feeling
loved by God—and not questioning it; Perfect Melancholies have
a need to know why.

One of my best friends is a Perfect Melancholy. She is always
asking me questions for which there is no reason I would know the
answer. (Scary thing is, I often do know.) One day she and I were
driving to her home in Pennsylvania when we came upon a detour.
All traffic was sent on a circuitous route. We drove and drove.
When we were in the middle of a cornfield with corn so high you
could see nothing else, she asked, "Where are we?" As if I would
know! But she seeks answers. Things I accept blindly, she wants to
know why.

> My child, listen to me and treasure my instructions. Tune your ears
> to wisdom, and concentrate on understanding. Cry out for insight
> and understanding. Search for them as you would for lost money or
> hidden treasure. Then you will understand what it means to fear the
> LORD, and you will gain *knowledge* of God. For the LORD grants
> wisdom! From his mouth come *knowledge* and understanding
> [Proverbs 2:1–6, NLT].

> He changes times and seasons; he sets up kings and deposes them.
> He gives wisdom to the wise and *knowledge* to the discerning
> [Daniel 2:21, NIV].

When we look at the definition of knowledge, it is truly something we should all strive to attain. But typically only the Perfect Melancholy is drawn to it. The Holman Bible Dictionary describes knowledge this way:

> The Bible speaks often about human knowledge. Knowledge of God is the greatest knowledge and is the chief duty of humankind. . . . This knowledge of God is not simply theoretical or factual knowledge; it includes experiencing the reality of God in one's life and living one's life in a manner that shows a respect for the power and majesty of God.

My father was a Perfect Melancholy. He loved to spend time digging in God's Word. He had numerous study helps and frequently used his concordances, Greek translation, and a variety of Bible versions. These study helps are favorites in the quest for knowledge.

Renee is a Powerful Choleric/Perfect Melancholy who has been involved in many teaching roles in her church. She says, "I love to get the facts, Scriptures, and details when preparing to teach at church. Sometimes to the point that there's no way I could teach it all in a day, much less the allotted hour." She says that a former pastor used to "caution" her to not get so caught up in obtaining so much knowledge that she forgot to let the Holy Spirit lead. She thought, *That's easily said, but hard to do for a Pefect Melancholy.* Later at a workshop, Renee heard another experienced teacher/speaker give a ten-to-one ratio as a guide for gathering knowledge on a topic. For every hour of teaching or speaking have at least ten hours of material, knowledge, or preparation behind it. Relieved, Renee says, "That one simple key freed me to once again enjoy digging deeply in the Bible, concordances, etc., and still have balance."

Like Renee, Peter enjoys digging for the facts and details. He wrote me to say that when he invited Jesus into his life, the first thing he did was to search the Scriptures to document and account for everything through the Bible until Jesus. It took him about two years of poring over the Scriptures, but he finally accomplished the goal. Then he put it all down on a timeline, added biblical characters, and developed a Bible study. He goes on: "The problem came in when I tried to teach it. First, I found most people were not interested in all these facts. Then I had to realize that with all this data, I am a dry and boring instructor—most of my students fell asleep." As you read that, if you are a Perfect Melancholy you may be asking, "Where can I get hold of Peter's study? That sounds fascinating."

The Perfect Melancholy is attracted to those vast amounts of knowledge, while the other personalities cannot understand why anyone would want to know all that just to take up brain space.

🍃 Powerful Choleric 🍃

When you think about the overall personality of the Powerful Choleric—whose motto mirrors "Just do it"—it is no wonder that the spiritual strength they embody is justification and works. Powerful Cholerics determine value—theirs and other's—on the basis of production. Likewise, they show their love for God through their works.

> But someone will say, "You have faith; and I have works. Show me your faith without your works, and I will show you my faith by my works" [James 2:18, NKJV].

> You foolish man, do you want evidence that faith without deeds is useless? Was not our ancestor Abraham considered righteous for what he did when he offered his son Isaac on the altar? You see that his faith and his actions were working together, and his faith was made complete by what he did. And the scripture was fulfilled that says, "Abraham believed God, and it was credited to him as righteousness," and he was called God's friend. You see that a person is justified by what he does and not by faith alone. In the same way, was not even Rahab the prostitute considered righteous for what

she did when she gave lodging to the spies and sent them off in a different direction? As the body without the spirit is dead, so faith without deeds is dead [James 2:20–26, NIV].

Because *justification* is not a word commonly found in our vocabulary today, we need to define it so we all understand this spiritual strength. Again, there is dispute as to the true meaning of the word. Because I am not trying to set a theological precedent but am instead attempting to show how the Powerful Choleric acts out his faith, I have cobbled together several elements that we will use here. The New Unger's Bible Dictionary offers a simple, clean definition of justification: "Justification is a divine act whereby an infinitely Holy God judicially declares a believing sinner to be righteous and acceptable before Him because Christ has borne the sinner's sin on the cross and has become 'to us . . . righteousness.'" It then goes on to say, "Throughout the whole history of this doctrine the principal point of difference and dispute has been as to whether faith is the only condition of justification or whether good works in connection with faith are also to be regarded as an instrumental cause." Adding to that, Easton's Bible Dictionary says: "Good works, while not the ground, are the certain consequence of justification." So, is it faith alone, or faith and works? I do not know, but I do know that for the Powerful Choleric, they are seen as one and the same.

For the Powerful Choleric, faith and works often combine in activism. These people are the ones who champion a cause. Years ago, Priscilla worked for me at CLASS (Christian Leaders, Authors and Speakers Services). She was a single mom who loved her daughter. There was no father on the scene, but Priscilla held a firm anti-abortion stand and was grateful that she had her child. With her background, Priscilla fully seized the pro-life platform. Because she so ardently believed in this cause, she felt everyone should. I remember having a heated discussion with her about it; she wanted CLASS to put a pro-life statement on every piece of literature that went out of our office. I do not disagree with the principle, but it is not what CLASS is about. I started CLASS to help train men and women to develop effective communication skills. Our mission statement is: "The complete service agency for both the established and aspiring Christian speaker, author, and publisher providing training, resources, and promotion." Clearly, a political stance is not a part of who we are. Hence I refused to add the pro-life statement and she was put out. She could not see how I would run a Christian organization and not take an activist stand.

From observations and conversations with people who have worked for him, I believe James Dobson is also a Powerful Choleric. The May 4, 1998, issue of *US News and World Report* featured a cover story on him. The article included these quotes from him: "I care about the moral tone of the nation. I care about right and wrong. I have very deep convictions about absolute truth. . . . I will fight that evil as long as there is breath within my body . . . I guess it irritates me when people who know what is right put self-preservation and power ahead of moral principle. That is more offensive to me, in some way, than what Bill Clinton does with interns at the White House. . . . It is never wrong to do what is right. And you stand for what's right whether it is strategic or not." Can you just hear the activist tone in those comments?

Jody, a survey respondent, adds that the best way to get a Powerful Choleric into church is through participation in a cause: "One of the largest areas [in which] I have seen Powerful Cholerics come to know God is through Habitat for Humanity. Actually building a home is a concrete way for Powerful Cholerics to serve God."

Bobbie has found that her faith and love for the Lord is exhibited in good works. Over the years, she has served by counseling those who could not afford to pay, worked in her church on multiple ministry teams, volunteered at and been president of the board for the Pregnancy Resource Center and codirector for the Women's Enrichment Ministry, and ministered to children in the Youth Detention Center. Yet she reports: "I always felt inferior about my spiritual life because I was falling short in my responsibilities to the Lord. No matter how hard I tried, I couldn't find one hour a day to worship with Him." Once Bobbie began to understand her spiritual personality, she realized that she was different from others and that is why God loves her. She knew she did not have to be like everyone else. She told me: "My way of sharing the Gospel and getting into the Word is by doing for others. This realization made me feel as though I had been set free." She goes on: "God knows my heart and He can see the fruits of my labor in His honor. I love my Lord and I am taking the skills He has provided me and am honoring Him just as He made me."

Clearly, the area of spiritual strength for the Powerful Choleric is justification and works.

❧ Peaceful Phlegmatic ❧

The Powerful Choleric wants to be in charge and make decisions. The Peaceful Phlegmatic is just the opposite, preferring to stay in the background and tending to be indecisive, hence easily accepting of the sovereignty of God.

> Moreover, because of what Christ has done, we have become gifts to God that he delights in, for as part of God's sovereign plan we were chosen from the beginning to be his, and all things happen just as he decided long ago [Ephesians 1:11, TLB].

> The God who made the whole world and everything in it is the Lord of the land and the sky. He does not live in temples built by human hands. This God is the One who gives life, breath, and everything else to people. He does not need any help from them; he has everything he needs. God began by making one person, and from him came all the different people who live everywhere in the world. God decided exactly when and where they must live [Acts 17:24–26, NCV].

I believe the sovereignty of God is a concept that is pretty easy to grasp. But since sovereignty is, again, not a word we use every day, let me call on the experts to explain its use here. Easton's Illustrated Dictionary simply defines the sovereignty of God as "His absolute right to do all things according to his own good pleasure." For the Peaceful Phlegmatic, this means God is in control; so why should I stress, why should I plan, why should I make a decision? In reality, the sovereignty of God is not that sweeping, but knowing God is in control is a comfort for the Peaceful Phlegmatic. Explaining it further, the Holman Bible Dictionary says:

> Divine sovereignty does not mean that everything which occurs in the world is God's will. God has created a world in which freedom is a real possibility. His permissive will provides for human freedom and the laws of nature. This freedom means that sovereignty must always be distinguished from "fate" or "destiny," the belief that everything which occurs in the world has been predetermined, scheduled in advance, by God. That view, carried to extremes, makes human beings pawns or puppets of a mechanical universe in which all choices are made in advance and where freedom is not possible. Yet the gospel suggests that human beings find genuine freedom, not in doing everything they wish, but in submitting themselves to the sovereign will of God, the rule and reign of God in their individual and collective lives. The sovereignty of God involves God's self-limitation in order that His creation might also choose freedom in Him.

With this in mind, we can see that the Peaceful Phlegmatic functions with a *que sera, sera* attitude (whatever will be, will be).

One event specifically points to Sharen's Peaceful Phlegmatic personality. She tells this story: "While directing a drama for the youth, portraying the song 'Watch the Lamb,' by Ray Boltz, my friend Chris came to me and said, 'Wouldn't it be great if we could include a real lamb in the show? I think I can borrow one from my parents' friends.' Of course, I agreed and considered it to be a done deal. It was a wonderful way to depict the Lamb of God and minister through a real illustration."

Sharen continues: "Two days prior to the performance, Chris told me the trailer wasn't going to be available to transport the lamb in time. I knew that lamb was meant to be a part of this production, that God had provided it as a vital role in proclaiming His sacrifice. I never considered 'no' as an answer. I knew He would take care of it."

God did provide transportation for the white lamb, and it arrived ten minutes prior to its stage debut. Sharen's friend, frazzled from the whole ordeal, gleamed with delight as she watched the beautiful illustration of sacrifice come to life before her eyes and commented later that the ministry of the lamb went beyond the point of the drama. Her friend saw that God could be relied on, that He is in control. Sharen, on the other hand, learned that our personality types can reflect the attributes of God that others can't see and understand.

The husband of a dear Peaceful Phlegmatic friend of mine died of brain cancer. At dinner the week following the funeral, my friend and I were having a discussion that we later had to laugh about. Our conversation veered to an ongoing theological debate: had her husband gotten brain cancer and died as punishment from God for his sinful pre-Christian life (as some people implied)? Or had God allowed it? Or was it simply the result of living in a fallen world? We brought up the differing viewpoints, commented on what others said, and then shrugged. We closed our conversation on the topic by agreeing that greater theological minds than ours have battled this question for hundreds of years. Probably, we were not going to solve it that night. As a Peaceful Phlegmatic, she was able to let go of the cause of her husband's death and move on.

I shared this story while speaking on the topic of spiritual personality. Afterward several Perfect Melancholies came up to me, wanting to discuss the "cause" issue. They wanted to share their opinion, rehash the topic, and come up with a solution. It bothered them that we had just gone "Oh well" on a topic of such importance. To a Perfect Melancholy, there must be a perfectly logical reason.

Spiritual Strength

Grace

And if He chose them by grace, it is not for the things they have done. If they could be made God's people by what they did, God's gift of grace would not really be a gift.
Romans 11:6 (NCV)

And all need to be made right with God by His grace, which is a free gift. They need to be made free from sin through Jesus Christ.
Romans 3:24 (NCV)

Justification/Works

But someone will say, "You have faith; and I have works. Show me your faith without your works, and I will show you my faith by my works.
James 2:18 (NKJV)

You foolish man, do you want evidence that faith without deeds is useless? Was not our ancestor Abraham considered righteous for what he did when he offered his son Isaac on the altar? You see that his faith and his actions were working together, and his faith was made complete by what he did. . . . You see that a person is justified by what he does and not by faith alone. . . . As the body without the spirit is dead, so faith without deeds is dead.
James 2:20–26 (NIV)

Sovereignty of God

Moreover, because of what Christ has done, we have become gifts to God that he delights in, for as part of God's sovereign plan we were chosen from the beginning to be his, and all things happen just as he decided long ago.
Ephesians 1:11 (TLB)

The God who made the whole world and everything in it is the Lord of the land and the sky. He does not live in temples built by human hands. This God is the One who gives life, breath, and everything else to people. He does not need only help from them; he has everything he needs. God began by making one person, and from him came all the different people who live everywhere in the world. God decided exactly when and where they must live
Acts 17:24–26 (NCV)

Knowledge

My child, listen to me and treasure my instructions. Tune your ears to wisdom, and concentrate on understanding. Cry out for insight and understanding. Search for them as you would for lost money or hidden treasure. Then you will understand what it means to fear the LORD, and you will gain knowledge of God. For the LORD grants wisdom! From his mouth come knowledge and understanding.
Proverbs 2:1–6 (NLT)

He changes times and seasons, he sets up kings and deposes them. He gives wisdom to the wise and knowledge to the discerning.
Daniel 2:21 (NIV)

Grace, knowledge, justification or works, and acceptance of Divine sovereignty are all evidence of our Christian life. All are good and valid. All are scriptural. Yet, depending on our spiritual personality, we manifest one spiritual strength more obviously than the others (see the figure given here). Nevertheless, all are needed. Perhaps this is what God meant by one body with many parts.

> The body is one unit and yet has many parts. As all the parts form one body, so it is with Christ. By one Spirit we were all baptized into one body. Whether we are Jewish or Greek, slave or free, God gave all of us one Spirit to drink. As you know, the human body is not made up of only one part, but of many parts. . . . So God put each and every part of the body together as he wanted it. How could it be a body if it only had one part? So there are many parts but one body. An eye can't say to a hand, "I don't need you!" Or again, the head can't say to the feet, "I don't need you!" The opposite is true. The parts of the body that we think are weaker are the ones we really need. . . . God's purpose was that the body should not be divided but rather that all of its parts should feel the same concern for each other. If one part of the body suffers, all the other parts share its suffering. If one part is praised, all the others share in its happiness. You are Christ's body and each of you is an individual part of it [1 Corinthians 12:12–27, GW].

Chapter Seven

Growing Closer to God

I find solace in places I never could have imagined
. . . the quiet sprinkling of my child's head in
Baptism, a gospel choir drunk on the Holy Spirit in
Memphis, or the back of a cathedral in Rome
watching the first cinematographers play with light
and colour in stained glass stories of the Passion.
I am still amazed at how big, how enormous a love
and mystery God is—and how small are the minds
that attempt to corral this life force into rules and
taboos, cults and sects. Mercifully, God transcends
the church.

—Bono, *quoted in* Good News,
July-August 2002, p. 40

As we have seen, each personality approaches spiritual life in its own way. The key principle is that understanding my spiritual personality helps me realize *why* certain spiritual exercises always come easier and make more sense to me; understanding my spiritual personality should *not* be used as an excuse to ignore my spiritual life. It is important for all of us to develop our spiritual life and grow closer to God. However, as we have seen, for some of us many of the popular methods produce more spiritual guilt than spiritual growth.

I believe we all acknowledge that we desire to grow in our spiritual life, and as Christians we want to be in a closer relationship with God. But what works for one person may not work for another. Let's look at what works for you, on the basis of your spiritual personality.

Study what has worked for others who share your basic spiritual personality and try the techniques that have worked for them. Stepping outside of the box adds variety to your routine and is almost sure to lead to progress in your spiritual life.

✿❧ Popular Sanguine ✿❧

Our research shows that Popular Sanguines are the people most discouraged about their spiritual life. Not that they don't feel close to God; they most feel like a failure because the "systems" do not work for them. If you draw a diagonal line through the squares in our figure, from the top right to the bottom left—through the Powerful Choleric and the Peaceful Phlegmatic—and then think about the presently popular programs for Bible reading, study, and prayer, you will see that they are designed for those to the bottom and right of that line: those with some portion of the Perfect Melancholy and either part Powerful Choleric (which gives the drive to follow through) or part Peaceful Phlegmatic (who appreciate the structure and system). For the Popular Sanguine—who inherently struggles with routine, these systems add frustration rather than faith.

For this reason, the number one piece of advice for the Popular Sanguine who desires to grow closer to God is, Don't give up! Like most of my Sanguine readers, I have tried over and over to follow through with those read-the-Bible-in-a-year plans. I have attempted the ones that my church handed out, in little brochures with a checklist telling you which Scriptures to read each day. I have tried the Bibles that do the work for you and divide the readings into daily sections. I have even tried the programs that suggest reading some of the Old Testament, New Testament, Psalms, and Proverbs each day. I know people who do this and it works great for them. But no matter how many times I have tried, I have yet to make it through the Bible in a year. I get to March and still have not finished January's assignment. I get so discouraged and feel like such a failure that I give up, thinking I'll try again next year. Reading a bit of each portion of the Bible left my poor pea brain confused.

I once had the opportunity to speak at a women's retreat where all they wanted me to speak on was the personalities. On Sunday morning, I spoke on the topic of this book, spiritual personality. By then each of the women in attendance had taken a Personality Profile (like the one found in the Appendix of this book) and had been a part of discussion groups. They had a good idea of their personality. I asked how many in the group found that they were at least 50 percent Popular Sanguine. About a quarter of the group raised their hands. I then asked, "How many of you who know you are at least 50 percent Popular Sanguine have read the Bible through in a year?" Even though I teach this material regularly, even though I know it well and knew what to expect for the answer, I was still surprised with the response. Not one of the Popular Sanguine Christian women at a church retreat raised their hands.

Wow! And this is marketed as what all good Christians do? No wonder the Popular Sanguine feels second class spiritually.

I comforted the group by saying, "I have read the entire Bible, not in a year, and I can tell you that nowhere in it does it say that we have to read the entire thing in a year." Every time I mention this, I am amazed at how many people come up and whisper that they have felt the same way: ashamed and less of a Christian because they were unable to do it.

Pam, a Popular Sanguine pastor's wife, shared her shame over not being able to fit the mold. She had attended a large seminar in which the main speaker cheerfully spelled out her orderly program, one of at least an hour of written prayer and Bible reading—daily; it even had a to-do list. There were books on prayer, and special journals for recording the hour spent with God. Every detail was organized to ensure success. Pam shared with me: "After a substantial financial investment—after all, I, too wanted success—I spent the next year and a half teaching these methods at my women's Bible study. I felt so drained and defeated with my own inability to keep up, to measure up. I certainly didn't want to admit that the program in which I had encouraged my women's ministry to get involved—the answer to our quest for higher spiritual ground—wasn't something I could keep up with. How could I expect them to do something in which I as the leader had failed?"

This does not mean that we should give up on reading the Bible. We do need to read it; it is a primary way we grow closer to God. It just doesn't need to be within a year's time frame.

One tool I have found that works especially well for me, and many other Popular Sanguines, is a particular edition called *The Narrated Bible*. You may not need another Bible, but here's why I like this one. First, it is narrated; throughout the text—in a different color ink—is the narration that tells you about the culture and the times, and it often draws your attention to an interesting fact you might have missed otherwise. It helps explain what is going on and makes your reading more interesting.

For example, having grown up in the church, I knew the story from Sunday school about the golden calf. I knew that Moses went up on the mountaintop and while he was gone left his brother Aaron in charge. Aaron built the golden calf (which created a wonderful pictorial for our child's Sunday school class). As an adult I read about the tabernacle and knew that God had appointed Aaron, Moses' brother, as the high priest. I knew these two items as fact. But until I read the "narration" I never connected that these two "Aarons" were one and the same. The narration commented on the fact that God forgave Aaron for building the golden calf and made him the spiritual leader of the nation of Israel. It then asked something to the effect of, "Have any of you done anything worse than leading an entire nation away from God? Couldn't God forgive you and use you?" A simple observation, but one I had never made on my own. The narration made the reading more interesting for me, so I kept with it.

The second thing I like about *The Narrated Bible* is its arrangement in chronological order. This means that, as far as the theologians know, the text is in the order in which events took place. For example, when reading through the Bible, many start at the beginning. They have no trouble with Genesis and Exodus, because they are stories. Then they hit Leviticus. All those laws are boring for most of us to read. But just as parents do not sit down one night and say, "Let's make a bunch of rules," neither did the lawmakers of Israel. Things happened that created a need for the law. In *The Narrated Bible*, the laws are placed within the context of when they were made. Instead of being a bunch of dull laws, they take on new meaning when read with the event that brought the rule into being.

Also, the Psalms are moved to the story with which they are connected. The Psalms for which the author is unknown or to which there is not a specific event connected are grouped by topic. You read the history of Israel and Judah together in Kings and Chronicles, as a parallel history. In the New Testament, the four Gospels are merged.

The third element of this Bible that I have found helpful for Popular Sanguines is the daily readings. *The Narrated Bible* is divided into 365 daily readings, but they are undated. This means you can start anytime; you do not have to wait until January. The best part is, if you get behind in your reading, you don't know that—so you keep reading as you can. If you are a Popular Sanguine and you have ever had trouble reading through the Bible, I suggest you check out *The Narrated Bible*. (Even many of my Perfect Melancholy friends have found this to be a helpful tool; it has offered a fresh new approach to their annual Bible reading.) Don't give up!

Another technique that works well for most Popular Sanguines is to be involved in a small group study. This gives us the accountability we need; to save face, we will read the verses and do the homework. For years I have attended a weekly Bible study at my church. The study takes place on Tuesday. The homework is structured to be done in twenty or thirty minutes per day. A diligent, dedicated person would do the homework as designed—a bit each day. But, when do you think I do it? Monday night. I schedule a couple of hours on Monday night to do that week's study. If I did not have the accountability of the small group, when would I do it? Never! I'd keep planning to and promise myself I'd get to it tomorrow—and tomorrow never comes. Fortunately, the facilitator of the group I am in understands this about me and does not reprimand me that I do not follow the rules. She encourages me. If I were put down for doing the study in my own style, I am sure I'd quit going.

If you are a Popular Sanguine and are not currently in a group study, I encourage you to find one. It may take trying out a few before you find the one that fits you best. You might check in at your local Christian bookstore to see if they know of any groups that are starting up or accepting new members.

If you are leading a study, please remember to be encouraging to the Popular Sanguines—whether or not they follow the rules, or even do the homework at all. It takes practice and discipline for the Popular Sanguine, and they do better in a loosely structured group. Addressing Bible studies, Judy said, "I have struggled with Bible study formats and consistency. I have tried those that have charts to figure out the what, why, when, etc., and those with thirty-five to forty-five minutes a day of looking up verses and doing the homework. I do not do well with them. Good as they are, I break down after a week and feel like a failure."

If you cannot find a Bible study group that meets your needs, why not start one? You do not need to feel qualified to teach since there are many wonderful studies out there that require only someone to facilitate; the book does the teaching. Many include a leader's guide as well. Post a notice at church or local Christian bookstore, or send invitations to all your friends. Even if only three people come regularly, there is nothing more motivating than having people arriving at your home at a specified hour for you to lead them, to make you get the study done. You only have to stay one lesson ahead of the group.

Accountability and participation are the keys for the Popular Sanguine.

I have heard it said, "I seldom spend fifteen minutes talking to God, but I seldom spend fifteen minutes without talking to Him."

This quote reflects the prayer life of the Popular Sanguine. Most of us do not do the scheduled, written prayers, but we talk to God all day long—after all, we Sanguines are talkers and He is our best friend. My girlfriends understand when I call them on my cell phone as I drive across town and have no one to talk to. They accept that I talk to them using my headset telephone while I am cooking dinner. Likewise, God hears my prayers and talks to me while I am driving, cooking, doing dishes, and folding laundry. None of these activities require my brain, or at least not all of it, so I multitask and pray.

Judy, AKA Hugs the Clown, reports: "I talk to God all day and most days spend time in prayer. I have tried all kinds of prayer-aids, lists of people and concerns for prayer, prayer books with pictures, etc." She realizes that as well-intentioned as these tools are, they have yet to work for her. She has been doing research on prayer to find a way that works for her and says, "I'm still searching and struggling to find a way to be more consistent." Judy, how much more consistent could you be than talking to God all day? You do pray. Embrace it.

After learning about her spiritual personality, Laurie sent me an e-mail with her experience. If, like her, you are a Popular Sanguine, I believe you will glean from her insights.

Laurie said she felt an indescribable relief, and then curiosity that perhaps, just maybe, she wasn't as shallow and unspiritual as she had always thought.

Over the years, Laurie says she had become a black-and-white thinker. Mistakenly, she felt she really didn't know how to worship God, because she didn't do it like everyone else. She told me, "I thought *this box* was the way to do it, and nothing else counted." Here's what Laurie's box looked like: "Go to church every Sunday (never miss!) and read your Bible—the longer, the better! And you'll get bonus points if you go to Wednesday night prayer meetings." Of course, there is nothing wrong with this plan. But Laurie wasn't leaving room in her worship for the way God created her. She says, "Up to this point, my idea of worship needed to fit someone else's box, the box created by someone who *really* knew how to worship God, because I knew I certainly didn't."

Laurie began a journey of rediscovery by asking herself, "When do I feel closest to God?" The answer was easy. She realized it was when she is in the midst of His nature—mountains, sunsets, seashells, birds. The answer had come up quickly, but her astounding realization was that even though she always thanked God for His majesty while enjoying nature, she never counted it as a major role or thrust in her worship experience. She expresses it this way: "In all reality it was my *impetus,* and I didn't realize it, because it didn't fit in the box."

Laurie continues: "As I focused on my spiritual personality, you suggested that most Popular Sanguines (my primary personality), because of their love for talking, have no trouble praying to God— usually in little sentence prayers [a line of prayer here or there as the thought arises]. However, they faltered in the listening area. I thought about that . . . it was true: I was not a good listener. Perhaps I should work on that. But I wasn't a good pray-er, either." She decided to give this listening thing a try to see what God would tell her when she gave Him a chance. She went outside (the nature thing, remember?), sat down, began her prayer, and just listened. "Immediately," she says,

> God brought back a memory that I hadn't thought of in years. I was transported back to when I was about ten years old. I was at my grandmother's house and praying to God for His help over a trivial thing. I remember chastising myself for bothering Him over something so inconsequential. Up to this point in my childhood, I had prayed to God constantly—in little sentence prayers! But as I matured, I stifled the very thing—God's design for me—that brought me to "saving up" for the important prayers. I did this so effectively, I had completely erased this "immature" way of praying from my thinking!

As she finished her prayer, she made up her mind to begin her sentence prayers again. Sure enough, Laurie would catch herself saying, "I've got to pray about this or that," and then put it on the back burner for an "official time of prayer." She began to ask herself, *Why not now?* and reminded herself, *It worked for me.*

A short time later, Laurie wrote this in her journal:

> Welcome back. Thank you, God. I know, it's been a long while. What's it been? I was somewhere between eight and twelve, when I chided myself for talking to You all day about nothing. About: "God, help me not to trip over the rug." I was at my grandmother's house and I believe that was the last straw. I had decided I was mentally going nuts with all those little sentence prayers going up to You all day long. Even though I told my friends you were never too busy for their prayers, I didn't believe it for myself—at least not asking for your help in not tripping over the rug. Oh boy—I had stopped, put a cork in, the very way that is natural for me to communicate with You. Wow. And I didn't even know it! I thought I had to sound like everyone else! If anyone would have ever asked if I compare myself to others, I would say no. I have no problem being my own individual. I also knew that God would hear our prayers, no matter our style. I knew it, I believed it—in my head. But I didn't understand it in my heart, until now. Thank you, Lord.

As Laurie stated it, "In the name of 'growing up', I was denying myself the very things I needed to draw close to God!" She gave me a list of what she was not doing. She was not listening. She was too busy doing. She would long to go outside to feel His presence, but would refrain because it sounded too much like play. She had long ago denied herself little sentence prayers, which were natural for her. So she developed an action plan for change. She would begin to notice when she felt close to God and do that more, even if it didn't fit the "prescribed way." She counted it as a way of spending time with God. She revitalized her sentence prayers and counted them. She noticed what she was lacking (listening) and made time for it in her day. Her relationship with God grew closer, and she wanted to read His Word more. She found a translation that worked for her (the Message). Finally, because of what she decided to do, she discovered how to worship and communicate in just the way God *made her!*

The final technique our survey respondents offered for the Popular Sanguines is Christian fiction. Though other personalities might turn their noses up at this as shallow and a waste of time, for the Popular Sanguine it is an excellent way to absorb biblical truth. It should not be the only source of spiritual growth, but a good novel written by a reputable author teaches passively.

Research has shown that when you read a personal growth book such as this one, or even the Bible, you read with your head. But when you read fiction, you read with your heart. The truth slips in there without your even realizing it. Today, there is a growing selection of good Christian fiction that—even though it is not teaching—often includes biblical lessons within the story and models a Christian approach to problem solving.

If you have not read Christian fiction lately, I suggest you try a few of my favorite authors: Gayle Roper, Jack Cavanaugh, James Scott Bell, and Doris Elaine Fell. I also belong to an inspirational book club called Heartsong Presents. Each month I get four Christian romance novels for around ten dollars—including shipping. I can read one in a few days without interrupting my life. I have several Popular Sanguine friends with whom I share them. We pass them around, and although we are all a bit ashamed to admit we like them, we do.

❦ Perfect Melancholy ❦

As noted, most Bible reading and study programs were created with the Perfect Melancholy in mind. The Popular Sanguine needs encouragement to keep at it; the Perfect Melancholy needs to relax!

In his classic devotional book *My Utmost for His Highest*, Oswald Chambers offers this caution, "Your god may be your little Christian habit, the habit of prayer at stated times, or the habit of Bible reading. Watch how your Father will upset those times if you begin to worship your habit instead of what the habit symbolizes—

I can't do that just now, I am praying; it is my hour with God. No, it is your hour with your habit. There is a quality that is lacking in you. Recognize the defect and then look for the opportunity of exercising yourself along the line of the quality to be added."

Pamela found that as a Perfect Melancholy this was a concern for her:

> I know if I were to say I must get up at 6:00 A.M. every morning to pray, I could, I would, and it would soon become meaningless, not at all genuine. I have a desire to always be genuine. I'm not afraid I won't be, it's just that I've known so many people who aren't. I don't want to be like them. They say you "must" do this or that. It seems that they "think less of your sincere devotion" if you don't have a daily routine. Routine for discipline's sake seems to nullify the sincerity of the act. I feel less connected to God if I try to follow such a rigid routine.

Because the Perfect Melancholy functions so well with a structured environment, it is easy to allow a time of Bible reading, for example, to be more about discipline and knowledge and less about God—more of a routine than a relationship. So, Perfect Melancholies, relax!

Teresa shared how her quiet time is "pretty structured." She wrote: "Sometimes I have to remind myself to lighten it up. My devotional time includes daily prayers. For this, I keep a prayer journal. I list specific things I pray about, with dates, and a large space to record my thoughts and feelings as I experience my prayers being answered, or questions about why I don't feel an answer." This allows Teresa to look back over a period of time and marvel at how God has worked and moved in her life. She says, "It also helps me learn that sometimes I'm simply not praying in ways that honor God; that my prayers are self-focused." As with many Perfect Melancholies, Teresa says that keeping a prayer journal relates well to the ability to analyze her prayer habits so they can be improved.

Teresa further comments: "There are times, though not frequently, when I write out prayers to God; these are usually dark, difficult times, when I pound the computer and type out long, heartfelt prayers." She says this was especially true several years ago, when she and her husband lost three of their four parents and a grandparent in less than five years. Reflecting back on this time, she says, "Somehow experiencing these prayers in the written word creates a powerful effect that brings some healing just in the doing of it."

Teresa states: "Since learning about the personalities, and my Perfect Melancholy tendencies, I have learned how to incorporate more spontaneity in my prayer life, and nothing ever 'waits to be prayed for' like it used to." She concludes by stating that although she still enjoys and needs the structured side of her prayer life, prayer is now as natural as breathing, and moves in and out of her day without pomp and circumstance.

Another tip for the Perfect Melancholy in growing closer to God is to allow ideals to be tempered with wisdom, knowledge, and compassion. In the search for knowledge, it is easy for the Perfect Melancholy to get wrapped up in reading books and attending seminars in search of the perfect way to do it. He or she can become absorbed with the technique and forget about God. What worked for Pamela may help you as well: "Take all the 'how to' specific instruction you receive and label it and put it on an imaginary shelf. Then go to God on your own, in prayer, and ask Him to help you find your own, personal unique way of relating with God—after all, that's what it's about. There is no one like anyone else. I repeatedly review all I have been taught, and prayerfully determine what/how to implement the good stuff, and build from there."

Continuing on the same theme, Pamela realized that she had to be forgiving of herself and others. "I have often been perplexed as to why others don't see the 'seriousness' of their behaviors or statements. Our personality type may be called 'perfect,' but it must be in terms of wanting things perfect—not because we are." Pamela has realized that she has very high standards; however, she has also learned that God is as forgiving and compassionate of her mistakes as He wishes her to be of others. Pamela concludes, "Instead of being a misfit and oversensitive as I'd been made to feel for all my growing up years, I can use my gifts in a positive way of influence and service."

So, relaxing and getting real are important tips for the Perfect Melancholy. Another key in the spiritual life of the Perfect Melancholy is to seek a quiet place. Because the Perfect Melancholy does not function well with multitasking, she needs a quiet place to commune with God. Barbara wrote, "Beautiful, peaceful surroundings, especially outdoors, make me feel close to God, particularly when I take the time to slow down and see the beauty he has provided."

Becky affirmed her need for a quiet place: "The scenario that brings me into His presence so quickly, is the majestic beauty of his creations—the heavens, the sun-lit clouds, the snow covered mountain peaks, the colors of the fall, the freshness of the spring and so much more. The touch of His hand is ever present . . . . the same hand that not only created all of nature, created me, and then endured the piercing of nails for me."

🌿 Powerful Choleric 🌿

As you may recall, both the Popular Sanguine and the Powerful Choleric, the top two squares on our chart, are outgoing and energized by people. So, even though the Perfect Melancholy does well developing the spiritual life in a quiet place with a quiet time, alone, the Popular Sanguine and the Powerful Choleric do well with people. The Popular Sanguine likes a group. The Powerful Choleric does not. The latter get frustrated with the typical pettiness of most small group settings, the mollycoddling that goes on, and the people who have to tell all about what they did last week. The Powerful Choleric is focused and always busy. They want to just get to the task at hand, not waste time—as they see it.

For the Powerful Choleric, a prayer partner or two is a good solution. For two years, two of my friends and I met together almost weekly—schedules permitting—to pray for our husbands and our marriages. We affectionately referred to our prayer time as "the praying wives club." All three of us had a large portion of Powerful Choleric in our personality mix. The hour-plus that we set aside to pray worked well for our schedules and our lives. With just three of us, we could be in control. We adjusted our meeting time to fit our needs rather than the static confinement of the usual Bible study.

Betty, whose personality is primarily Powerful Choleric, has a prayer partner with whom she has prayed for more than thirty-five years. A scheduled time of prayer—to talk about what is happening in their lives, the lives of their husbands, families, and friends—meets the Powerful Choleric's need for doing something.

As Betty described her experience, meeting with her prayer partner has opened her eyes to see things from a new perspective. Identifying, recognizing, and talking about various concerns or problems with her prayer partner have given direction to her prayer life. She said, "The process has opened me up to new insights. Sometimes I have to radically adjust my attitudes, actions, or expectations. Many times it is my prayer partner who sees things from a clearer perspective. She can ask gentle questions that may point out an attitude problem in me." According to Betty, another benefit of having a prayer partner is that speaking the words out loud to someone else often helps her hear what she was saying in a different way.

A prayer partner is a relationship where you come together as equals. It is not a mentoring relationship but is instead built on mutual trust and respect. It is something that grows rather than just happening. It takes time to build a relationship in which each person loves, trusts, and respects the other. There must be a desire to be honest, vulnerable, accepting, tolerant, and loving. There must also be a willingness to believe the best about each other.

Since control is a central issue for the Powerful Choleric, this can be a major hurdle in such a relationship. The Powerful Choleric needs to be aware of the tendency to want to control time, method, and outcome, not only with a prayer partner but in one's own private prayer life as well. If you are a Powerful Choleric, look to develop a prayer partner relationship with one or two people who share your desire to grow closer to God.

Another technique that works well for Powerful Choleric is to use short devotional books with clear concepts. Powerful Cholerics are busy people who have more to do in a given day than is humanly possible. They do not have the time for involved studies. But they do not like the little devotional books that tell a cute story and then have a brief biblical application stuck on the end. They want more meat. They do not want to feel they are wasting their time.

Elaine, who is about fifty-fifty Popular Sanguine and Powerful Choleric, responded with this comment about what works in growing closer to God: "So what has worked the best for me in providing the 'meat' I yearn for in developing a relationship of fellowship with God? Mine is a three-step devotional time." Elaine starts with a brief one- to two-page reading (or more, when time allows) in a devotional or Christian growth book. She looks for a sentence, phrase, or paragraph that has particular meaning to her and her life at that time (even if it is a word of encouragement for her to share with someone else that she'll meet or be talking to). She says, in an e-mail: "If it's a devotional book, you must understand that it is flipped open anywhere—who could follow a date order? Obviously, God isn't necessarily going to say the same thing to me on the date the writer set up. I want to be free to let God open the pages of my book and my Bible. (smile!)"

The second step of Elaine's devotional time is reading several verses or a chapter of Scripture until she hears God speaking to her through His Word, confirming what she read in the devotional book. She gives this tip: "And it's a very fun practice to put a date and place in the margin beside the verse that has special meaning. When we go back through our Bible or journal in future years, it becomes a time-line of the ways in which God has met with us."

Elaine's third step is journaling the devotional thought for the day; the Scripture verse(s) confirming God's Word to her; and a prayer of thanks, commitment, or worship, being sure to write down the promises and proclamations that she believes God is saying are for her at this time and situation in her life.

When asked, "Does it always work, and why?" Elaine's response is affirmative: "Because I have determined that I will not leave my quiet time until I have heard a Word from God. Some days it takes longer than others—usually because I am too distracted, too rushed, too impatient or otherwise occupied. But God is always there—waiting and ready to meet me, when I am finally quiet and ready to listen to Him speak."

For other Powerful Cholerics, Elaine offers suggestions for books that might be helpful in a time of devotions:

My Utmost for His Highest, by Oswald Chambers, updated ed., edited by James Reimann (Discovery House Publishers, 1992)

Dare to Journey with Henri Nouwen, by Charles Ringma (Pinon Press, 2000)

Starting Your Day Right: Devotions for Each Morning of the Year, by Joyce Meyer (Warner Faith, 2003)

Prayers to Move Your Mountains: Powerful Prayers for the Spirit-Filled Life, by Michael Klassen and Thomas Freiling (Thomas Nelson, 2000)

In a Quiet Place, by Jill and Stuart Briscoe (Shaw, 1997)

His Victorious Indwelling: Daily Devotions for a Deeper Christian Life, edited by Nick Harrison (Zondervan, 1998)

Powerful Cholerics are also the most goal-oriented of the personalities. Ida Rose found that for her it helped to set spiritual goals, not just human ones: "I tend to be very goal-driven, but my goals have not necessarily been God-inspired. I've had goals such as finishing my master's degree and then my doctorate, but until the last two years my spiritual goals have been either nonexistent or 'law-driven' (such as 'pray an hour every morning'). Now I find myself having goals like being focused on the Holy Spirit's leading when my four-year-old son is in the midst of his nightly suppertime temper tantrum." Ida Rose recently told me that her primary goal in life right now is to know Him. She still has other goals—such as placing ten articles for publication this year—but she is not nearly as driven by them and they are subjected to the greater goal of knowing Jesus and obeying Him.

The Perfect Melancholy seeks knowledge; the Powerful Choleric wants information—she just does not want to make a career of it. For the Powerful Choleric, Bible software is a great tool. With point-and-click ease, you can go deeper and deeper, spending more time in God's Word and supplemental materials than you'd ever think possible. Every time I use the software, I find myself wishing I had more time to develop my study further. When I sit in a chair or lie in my bed with my beautiful, heavy, leather Bible with tissue-thin pages, somehow I just want to go to sleep. The software, by contrast, makes it more interactive; I am participating, not just reading.

As with the basic personality of the Powerful Choleric, "doing" and "action" are central to this personality. Likewise the techniques that work best in developing a spiritual life are participatory, not passive.

🌿 Peaceful Phlegmatic 🌿

I believe the Peaceful Phlegmatic must be God's favorite personality. Yes, He made us all as we are, but the Peaceful Phlegmatic is the one who can "be" and who doesn't have to "do." Of the hundreds of people who responded to our surveys, the Peaceful Phlegmatic is the only group that indicated one of the tools that helped them in their spiritual life was to "ponder" Scripture. While the Popular Sanguines and Powerful Cholerics are buzzing around in busyness and the Perfect Melancholy is digging deeper, the Peaceful Phlegmatic is basking in God's presence.

Lindy Lou offered this advice to her fellow Peaceful Phlegmatics: "Don't be in hurry, ponder. I have a prayer notebook that a friend gave me. I've labeled one section 'Ponder Scripture.' I like to write out a verse or paragraph of Scripture, and ask God all kinds of questions. I try to visualize myself in the setting, look up the meaning of words in Strong's concordance, and try to see the nature of God and how to apply His word."

She also encourages Peaceful Phlegmatics to create some traditions or rituals:

> Every morning I go to my home office, open the drapes, light a candle, sing a song, sit in my little brown rocking chair, write out my prayers, and ponder scripture. On cool mornings, I wrap up in a lap quilt from my older sister and a soft blanket from my mother. My view is of bookcases, a tall, brass candlestick from my older sister, needlework pillow saying "Sisters are Friends Forever" from my younger sister. On top of the shorter bookcase, I have a small lamp with a handmade shade, a few precious-to-me books on letters, a framed Scripture *Be still and know that I am God* (Psalms 46:10). Through the window, I can see ivy on the wall, branches of a fig tree and the night change to day with each sunrise.

Although Peaceful Phlegmatics do well with set formulas and tradition, regimen has a tendency to paralyze them. Therefore, a tip for the Peaceful Phlegmatic is to make a commitment that is intentional, not legalistic. Vicky offered this comment about her husband: "Brian is a man of uncompromising character and integrity. He is a deeply committed Christian and a highly respected leader. However, he has difficulty with such things as Bible reading plans and Scripture memory systems. As a matter of fact, he is now on the second year of a Read-the-Bible-in-a-Year plan! Brian feels it is important to stay consistently in the Word and therefore continually attempts to stay true to a system of Bible reading. He says, 'I've always wished it would get easier, but it never has.'"

Pastor Steve, a Peaceful Phlegmatic himself, says, "My best advice for Peaceful Phlegmatics is to vary your routine." He further adds that you should not feel as though you are a failure because you do not have the same set time every day for study and prayer. He concludes: "We Peaceful Phlegmatics tend to enjoy the variety as long as we are consistently spending time with our Lord."

Learn from each other. Try the things that have worked for others of your same personality. You will find a renewed relationship with God as you do the things that help you draw closer to Him.

As Pam, the Popular Sanguine pastor's wife, shared with me, "What a freedom there is in receiving God's direction and blessing, knowing His plan is perfect and specifically for me." She says that "set free" seems to be a common emotion among all the personalities. There must always be room for growth, stretching, and knowledge. How we get there doesn't seem to matter—SUV, sports car, race car, or bus.

Chapter Eight

The Personality of Jesus

May thy grace, O Lord, make that possible to me
which seems impossible to me by nature.
—*Amy Carmichael, in* Magnificent Prayer
(ed. Nick Harrison)

As Christians most of us have been taught that we should aim to be like Jesus. We know that our goal is to be more like Him, that our lives should exhibit the Fruit of the Spirit. Yet for many this remains an abstract concept. However, when we look at Jesus Christ and His "church"—all of us, in light of the personalities—this principle takes on new clarity.

Being "like Christ" seems an ominous task, until we begin to look at the life of Christ as found in the Gospels and specifically focus on His personality. Now that we understand the basics of personality, we can understand how we can be more like Him when we study His life. If you were to do a personality profile on the life of Christ, you'd find that He has the strengths of all four personalities and the weaknesses of none. With the goal of being more Christlike, we do not use our own personality as an excuse to stay in our comfort zone; we use it as a tool to grow, mature, and become more balanced.

Here is what you'll likely find as you look at the life of Christ through the filter of the personalities.

❧ Popular Sanguine ❧

As we think of Christ through the personalities, we see that He was a Popular Sanguine; the very first miracle and encounter in His earthly ministry was at a party! There He performed the miracle of turning water into wine. Without His help the party might have dwindled, and it surely would not have been remembered thousands of years later. We could easily see that Christ was the life of the party.

In fact, everywhere Jesus went, there seemed to be a party. Even the circumstances surrounding His birth became a party, with people coming from far and wide to attend. There was a heavenly light show, and even presents! Popular Sanguines have that same quality; their very presence can turn any event into a party. They do not have to know people to bring them into the group. Their charm and openness attract total strangers, who join in on the activities or else eavesdrop from the sidelines wishing they were bold enough to jump into the action. Popular Sanguines often refer to these people as their "new best friends." Everywhere Christ went, throngs of people followed Him. With the magnetism of the Popular Sanguine, Jesus called "follow me" and people did. Crowds of people sat on hillsides and listened to His stories. Groups stood on the shores and hung on every word. He held his audiences spellbound as He shared with them parables of common things and delighted them with His stories—always leaving them wanting more.

Jesus was an optimist. Jesus says that if we have faith, all things are possible (Mark 9:23). Jesus spoke of the dead daughter of a synagogue official and said that she was not dead, only sleeping (Matthew 9:19–24).

Jesus did not have the vast clothing options we have today, but it is clear that, like a Popular Sanguine, He was not afraid to stand out in the crowd. Much of His ministry took place on mountain tops, rooftops, in synagogues, and on the streets. In John 18:20, Jesus acknowledges that He has spoken openly; and in John 18:8, He steps to the front, acknowledging who He is.

Physically, Popular Sanguines seem to have an unlimited supply of energy that they can call into service as needed. As we look at the life of Christ, and especially study a map of Bible lands, we see that He had amazing strength. The geography covered by Christ in His three short years of ministry shows He could outlast most of us today.

Yes, Jesus was definitely a Popular Sanguine.

🌿 Powerful Choleric 🌿

Yet Jesus also shows many strengths of the Powerful Choleric. Certainly He was a born leader. No other world leader has had such an impact as to have all of time marked by his presence by most of the world's population! He was goal-oriented and purposeful. Christ knew why He had come to earth, and everything He did was to meet that end. In John 8:14, He says, "I know where I came from and I know where I am going." Such purpose and confidence positioned Him to preach in the synagogue at a young age. Satan tried to tempt Him with many exciting possibilities during His stay in the wilderness—all of which fit His talent, yet none of which fit his purpose or His goals. He turned them all down, staying focused on the job He was called to do.

Like a Powerful Choleric, Christ was a man of action, not just an observer on the sidelines. He boldly went into the temples and turned over the tables of the money changers. He transformed water into wine. He prepared a meal for thousands. The list could go on and on. Even John could not catalogue all of Christ's activities. At the conclusion of His written record of Christ's life, John said there was no way to capture all of the things which Jesus did; to do so would require more books than the entire world could hold (John 21:25). As a man of action, Jesus did not often stop to rest. In John 5:17 He said, "My Father is working . . . I myself am working."

Christ was not afraid of a good fight. He thrived on opposition. He reminds us that He did not come to bring peace to the world, but rather a sword (Matthew 10:34).

Powerful Cholerics also like to get right to the point. They do not want to hear all the details or all the excuses. They are interested in the facts. So was Christ. When the Pharisees came to Him asking for advice on which of the laws was the most important, Jesus got right to the point and said, "You shall love the Lord your God with all your heart, with all your soul and with all your mind . . . You shall love your neighbor as yourself." In two brief sentences he captured the bottom line of all the laws (Matthew 22:37).

The Gospels are full of incidents where Christ delegated authority. In the feeding of the five thousand, His disciples came to him with what they saw as an insurmountable problem. Jesus quickly assessed the situation, since it didn't allow planning or committee meetings, and told the men how to take care of the problem. Under His authority, He sent the disciples out to heal the sick. To each of us He delegated the responsibility of bringing in the harvest when He said (in Matthew 9:37) "The harvest is plentiful but the laborers are few."

Yes, Jesus was a Powerful Choleric.

🌿 Perfect Melancholy 🌿

Certainly anyone who knows anything about Jesus Christ would not deny that He was a Perfect Melancholy. After all, He was "perfect"! Not only was Christ perfect Himself, He encouraged the same qualities in us (Matthew 5:48). He was clearly a planner and organizer. When Jesus commissioned His disciples, He didn't just send them out. He gave them full and detailed instructions, including which type of cities to visit, what kind of money to carry, and what specific clothing to wear (Matthew 10:1–23). Christ had a plan of His own that he was to follow. He frequently spoke of things being part of that plan, including His death.

Jesus also appreciated time alone. He often recharged his batteries with the solitude of the garden, the desert, or the mountaintop. After a very busy day, Jesus liked to spend time alone in prayer on a mountaintop (Matthew 14:23). In Mark 1:35 Jesus was in a "solitary place" when Peter and the others were anxiously looking for Him. As Christ's popularity increased and great multitudes flocked to Him, he often withdrew to the wilderness (Luke 5:15, 16, Mark 6:1). We know that when the soldiers arrested him, He was in the garden (Matthew 26:36). He had been in the wilderness for forty days and nights when Satan tempted him. Imagine a Popular Sanguine spending forty days and nights alone.

Like the Perfect Melancholy, Christ was caring, sensitive, and emotional. He looked out for the social outcasts, and the untouchables—the lepers, the Gentiles, the sinners—and he cared for them. In Mark 1:40, we read that Jesus took pity on a leper. He blessed the prostitute and forgave her sins. He instructs us that not even one little sheep should perish because all are important. He cared for the little children. Mark 10:16 tells us that He "took the children into His arms and placed His hands on their heads and blessed them" (TLB). The Bible verse all children love to memorize because it is the easiest, John 11:35, simply tells us that "Jesus wept." He was not afraid of tears or emotion.

The Perfect Melancholy is genius-prone. At only twelve years old, Jesus was wise beyond His years and spent time teaching in the synagogues.

Truly, Jesus reflected the qualities of the Perfect Melancholy.

🌿 Peaceful Phlegmatic 🌿

As we look at the strengths and qualities of Christ, we see many skills the world applauds. He was popular. He was a great leader. He was organized. However, a thorough search of Christ's character reveals an abundance of traits for which few people strive. But within them lies the true essence of Christlike behavior. He was a man of service. He had compassion. He was willing to do the lowly task. He wasn't so busy with accomplishment that he forgot to smell the roses. He played with the children. He held the hand of a little girl. He grieved with a family. He was fair. He took time to look people in the eye and love them. He was humble. He took time to notice the lilies swaying in the wind—and admonished us to do the same ("consider the lilies of the field"). He told us to treat everyone we meet with value, as though they are the children of God. Which personality has all of those attributes? None other than the Peaceful Phlegmatic. Now you know why Jesus was known as the Prince of Peace!

Christ took the time to serve, even through the lowly task of washing the feet of the disciples. In doing so, He used his own clothing to dry their feet and instructed us to follow His example. He tells us the first shall be last and the last shall be first.

Jesus was fair to all. He came to set the captives free; He came as the Messiah for the Jews. Yet He reached out to everyone, the healthy and the sick, the Jews and the Gentiles, the men and the women. We have already seen how Christ touched the untouchables. We know that He conversed with the rich (Mark 10:22, Matthew 19:16–23) and the educated (Matthew 12:9–10, Matthew 8:5–6, Luke 2:46–47). Interestingly, among the first and last recorded events in Christ's life are those involving women. Of course, it was Mary who brought Him into the world. The angel of the Lord spoke directly to Mary, telling her to "be not afraid." After Christ's resurrection, women were the first to recognize Jesus. They were instructed to go and tell the others (Matthew 28:1–10). Jesus was certainly fair to everyone.

In the story of the rich young man in Mark 10, we see that Jesus took time to look people in the eye—not just a quick passing by, but long enough to be moved by them and their needs. Verse 21 tells us that Christ *looked* at him and *felt* a love for him.

When we look at the life of Christ, we must agree that He was a mighty man. He did many wonderful things, and He was a great person. Jesus had many reasons why He might view Himself as a king, someone to be worshiped. Yet He did the lowly things; He served and He was humble. In John 14:12, Christ tells us that although He does great things, anyone who believes in Him can do also—even greater.

Clearly Christ was and is a Peaceful Phlegmatic, the Prince of Peace.

Jesus had all the personality strengths and none of the weaknesses. He had a perfectly blended personality that reflected his Father. He said, "When you have seen me, you have seen the Father." He came to be an example for us, that we might be like him and please the Father—who, as we have seen in Chapter Four, also has elements of each personality.

Becoming Like Christ

As we understand the personalities and the personality of Jesus, becoming more like him is made clear. Our personality is our raw person. It is who we naturally are. As the Holy Spirit shapes us, we begin to lose those rough edges of our personality—the weaknesses—and through the power of the Holy Spirit we can take on the strengths of some of the other personalities that are not natural to us.

Cathy has done this in her life. What she has learned about the personalities, and knowing that Jesus was a combination of the strengths of all four personalities and none of the weaknesses, is that she has a roadmap of how to become more like Christ. She said that she looks at the list of strengths for the various personalities and then tries to take those on, not all at once of course. As a Popular Sanguine/Peaceful Phlegmatic, Cathy states, "I have striven to become more organized and detail-oriented, like the Perfect Melancholy. Never being a goal setter, I am learning to set goals and keep myself accountable to them. Those are just some of the areas. Jesus told stories, but did not get sidetracked like we Popular Sanguines seem to do, going off on tangents, and boring people to death."

Ultimately, as we work on our personality, we become more Christlike. This is why it is often difficult to identify the personality of someone who has been a Christian for many years, in whom the Holy Spirit has been dwelling, and who has made a conscious effort to be more like Christ. At this place in their life, they have become more like Him; they are more balanced and they now exhibit strengths that are not natural for them.

Bobbie has had to work to learn skills that are not natural to her. As a Popular Sanguine, she finds her church calls on her frequently to handle meetings and events or just to speak with people—something she really enjoys doing. She has learned, however, that not everything can be a party. There are times she must turn herself into a Perfect Melancholy or a Peaceful Phlegmatic. She says, "This can be very difficult for me; however, with deep prayer and guidance from the Holy Spirit, I am able to add that balance. While I love to work on events, I find I must follow a schedule or the event may not happen on time. I also must ensure that every detail is exact and followed as planned or the entire event can be jeopardized."

As a counselor, Bobbie has had to learn to get deep with individuals and be highly sensitive to their needs and hurts. She says, "As I do this I must be cautious and not try to make light of what someone is going through. I have had to learn to listen and not talk . . . do you know how difficult that is for a Popular Sanguine? I am so thankful that God has provided me the courage and strength to be able to move into different styles when the need arises." Bobbie did admit to me that overall she is always happy to get back to her natural style of being a Popular Sanguine/Powerful Choleric.

This is the case as well for Shirley. She says, "As I read about the personality strengths and weaknesses, I can't help but marvel and be thankful that God can and does make changes in our personality." At age seventy-three, Shirley can certainly see that He has worked in her life. Her natural personality is a combination of the Popular Sanguine and Powerful Choleric, playful and headstrong. She realizes that through God's work in her life and trials, tragedies, and blessings, she now exhibits the traits of the Peaceful Phlegmatic, submissive and peaceful. Shirley asks, "Can we say that

all roads lead to Rome, that all personalities lead to being con-
formed to the image of Christ?" I certainly agree with Shirley that
the answer to this question is, Yes, all personalities do lead to the
image of Christ.

When we accept Jesus Christ as our Savior, we take on a new
life. Ephesians 4:20–24 tells us we are to "put off former conduct,
the old man . . . and be renewed in the spirit and mind." Colossians
3:10 states that we are renewed in His image.

Teresa found that when she worked on it, she and her friends
were able to begin adapting their personalities and taking on that
renewed image. She reports that she has been involved with a
weekly accountability group for about five years; she meets with
three other women every Tuesday evening in one of their homes,
for the purpose of sharing, praying together, providing accountability, and helping each other to grow spiritually.

Teresa shared with me that, a couple of years ago, they had their
own little "personality party," where the personalities were intro-
duced and they all took the Personality Profile. This experience has
caused them much discussion and growth over the past couple of
years. What they found was that with all four in the group, they
make up a perfect combination: one is Peaceful Phlegmatic/Popular
Sanguine, one is Popular Sanguine/Powerful Choleric, one is Perfect
Melancholy/Powerful Choleric, and one is Peaceful Phlegmatic/
Perfect Melancholy. What a group!

Teresa continues: "Many times, as we encourage one another
in spiritual growth, we are able to learn from one of the others in
the group about how to respond/react differently, in a way that is
not natural to our own personality. It takes persistence and practice, but eventually we find ourselves thinking and acting differently in situations, and we all celebrate what we are learning from
each other through our differences, and through our knowledge of
the personalities."

It is not that our personality changes or that we lose whom God
originally created us to be, but rather that we become complete in

Him—the abundant life He promised, full and overflowing. When we are complete, the world notices something different in us; people see Jesus Christ in our lives.

So as we grow and mature, how does that change our spiritual personality? It means we begin to see and experience the bigger picture. Our relationship with God takes on new depth and understanding. We begin to see others through the eyes of a loving and just Father, which gives us the ability to be merciful and forgiving.

View of God

In Chapter Four we looked at how each us, on the basis of our natural personality, automatically responds to certain elements of God's character. But as we grow and mature, we see the full spectrum of who He is. Jan found this to be the case within her family. Jan shared with me that as a Popular Sanguine her view of God is that she is constantly looking for His approval, and her relationship with Him is always a whirlwind. She writes, "Most of my family members are Peaceful Phlegmatics and I have learned so much about God from them. They see God as constant, and never changing. They rely on God's capacity to always be approving, never out there blowing with the wind and changing His mind. They know He is never asking them to do more than they can deliver, and they are not volunteering to do more than they can deliver."

Jan observes, "I watch how they worship, quiet, without fanfare, but deep and abiding. They never get flustered with God, and they truly believe He never gets flustered with them. There is a deep steadfastness about their approach. They are content to sit on the sidelines in church and, like Jesus, be the 'silent servers.' They always find a place of peace with God."

In contrast, Jan's son-in-law is a Powerful Choleric. She says he is always frustrated and truly believes God to be frustrated with us. He asks, "Why can't we do it perfectly and do it perfectly the first time?" She shares, "He has so many compartments and boxes for each aspect of our Christian walk: prayer, the church service, giving, the Bible. He spends much of his time analyzing how everything could be done better and more efficiently. He never takes anything for granted and serves God with zeal and uncompromising standards. He does not just come in and out like the tide."

Jan continues with insight into her family: "Then our little band of believers are all tied together by my husband, the stalwart leader of this clan, the Perfect Melancholy. He always brings us into a place where it is action, not just words. It is commitment and faithfulness pushed to deeper and deeper levels. He never wavers because he knows 'whom he has believed in,' much like Abraham. He always goes back to the basics and a solid foundation of belief. He has taught us always to do the right thing instead of relying on our emotions."

Because of the examples of her wonderful family of believers, Jan says, "I am always challenged to be in peace, to be stable, constant, to be committed, to be faithful no matter what is going on around me. They are good role models for me to see all of God and His many faces not just from my prospective. I watch their lives and how God has blessed them and know that in God's economy there is room for each one of us at the foot of the cross. If it had been left to me it would have been all about just having fun!"

Worship Experience

Van acknowledges that her personality influences what she is most naturally attracted to in a church; she also admits that her behavior and criticisms grew from her selfish and sinful nature. For all of us, without the growth that comes about as we aim to be more Christlike, we seek to please our earthly desires.

As Van's spiritual life has matured, knowing her personality style has revealed her weaknesses to her and encouraged her to discipline herself: to look at worship, Bible study, church choice, and attendance as acts of obedience to her Lord and not just as a self-serving ritual to make her feel good. She says, "My relationship with Jesus is now about Him and His calling to me, not about my perceptions and desires to have life be designed for my comfort. That said, I realize that I still operate out of the flesh. It is not until I check myself, or it is brought to my attention, like a review of the personalities, that I realize the importance of setting Christ as my standard."

Spiritual Strength

In Chapter Six, we discussed the spiritual strength toward which each personality most naturally gravitates. Yet as we grow in Christ, we begin to take on the wider scope of the Christian life. We embrace elements of faith that we often struggle to accept.

We think of grace as the spiritual strength for the Popular Sanguine. But as Sheryl relates, being a mature Perfect Melancholy she has learned about grace.

She told me her story recently: "I was raised a Roman Catholic (and I was good at being a hard-working Catholic) and when I was a freshman in college I came to know the Lord through a theology course that required that I read the four Gospels weekly. It was this reading and some other events that brought me to Christ on a personal level. When I finally came to know Christ, I was keenly aware of what sin was even though my sinful ways did not involve drugs, alcohol or sexual immorality. But all of a sudden I had this keen awareness of sin and imperfection."

She continued: "It took me the first thirteen years of knowing Christ to get over fearing God, and anticipating a lightning bolt to come out of the sky and strike me down dead. Even though I went from a good works mentality to salvation by grace mentality, my head took forever to catch up with the fact that God loved me unconditionally and that God was a God of grace and mercy. I struggled so much with the fact that I was imperfect and with believing that God could love me 'Just as I Am.'"

So the concept of perfection, fearing God, and feeling she had to be perfect to be loved by God was entirely real to Sheryl. As she reveals, "It still haunts me today (not as severely) but study of Scripture, through church teaching, through personal study of many aids, such as Wilmington's Concordance and Strong's Concordance and many types of Bibles (NIV Study Bible, Thompson Chain Reference, King James, Ryrie Study Bible) has helped immensely." Sheryl says that she is enjoying her Perfect Melancholy personality in relationship with God, and that she is learning more and more about God's grace and no longer fears the lightning bolt from heaven. She concludes by saying, "I know more and more that God loves me, imperfections and all!"

Growing Closer

As Betty has grown in her relationship with Christ, she has found that the spiritual growth techniques she has successfully used for years were no longer as satisfying as they once were. She remembers that in earlier years of seeking she kept herself surrounded with noise. Good noise: Christian music, recordings of speakers, Christian radio programs—always on, while she worked around the house or ran errands in the car. When faced with silence, she always found some way to fend it off. Today she says she longs for silence and solitude. Betty has found she needs both time and space to ponder what God might be saying through His Word, the words of others, or the circumstances of her life.

For Betty, this transition has not been easy: "I have found it hard to shut out my thoughts, plans, or worries. I did what most Powerful Cholerics do when they decide they need to make some changes in their lives. I ran to the bookstore and bought books that would tell me how to accomplish this discipline. Same old Powerful Choleric determination: I will make this work! But it didn't."

Betty has found that she has to "escape" somewhere away from home in order to quiet herself enough to finally begin hearing God's voice. She confesses, "I am still working on giving myself permission to do nothing but sit and be silent at home. I still fight the need to do something measurable at every day."

Like most Powerful Cholerics who typically look for a way to measure productivity, Betty too finds that it is hard to measure what

God does in the silence and solitude of our hearts—especially at those times when it seems He does nothing. She is aware, however, that there is a subtle difference in her when she allows herself to experience a time of "intentional nothingness." She admits that "these times are molding and changing me, and I find myself yearning—in the midst of a too-busy schedule—for that time of silence and solitude."

As we look at the personality of Jesus and how His life modeled the best of everything for us, we can see how to grow and mature and bring more balance into our personality. When we surrender to Him, He begins to transform us into our authentic selves, removing the destructive parts of our weaknesses and moving toward Him. Oswald Chambers puts it this way: "One of the greatest hindrances in coming to Jesus is the excuse of our own individual temperament. We make our temperament and our natural desires barriers to coming to Jesus. Yet the first thing we realize when we do come to Jesus is that He pays no attention whatsoever to our natural desires."

Chapter Nine

Spiritual Personality and Spiritual Gifts

> A one-size-fits-all approach to spirituality doesn't work. Life situations and experience play an important role in forming one's spiritual commitment. Know your people, know their needs, and find ways to meet those needs person by person.
>
> —*Albert Winseman, quoted in* Baptists Today,
> *June 2002, p. 17*

If we are supposed to be like Christ, having some of all the personalities, why did He make each of us with such a distinct personality?

In the last chapter, we looked at how we can use our individual personality as a tool to become more Christlike as we each aim to take on strengths that are not natural to us, and work to prayerfully eliminate weaknesses. With that approach, we ultimately do become more balanced.

As individuals, we do want to be more like Christ, but when we look at the church as a whole, with all of the various personalities, we already have all of the strengths present—like Christ! As humans we also have the weaknesses, but when the Christian community comes together as one, we have all of the strengths as well. One body, with many parts. One vine, with many branches.

The Work of the Body of Christ

When we are all living spirit-filled lives and we come together in our strengths, we as a group are like Christ. This is how we, as Christians, are intended to function. No one has every skill or strength. But as we come together, we make a whole, complete in Him. Prior to discovering this, a survey respondent named Ellen says, "Being outgoing, as a Christian I used to judge shy believers as cold and unwelcoming to new converts I would bring into church. I didn't understand that people are gifted in different ways."

Whether the group we are referring to is the entire Christian community, a specific church body, a parachurch organization, or a group of Christians banding together in a specific cause, we are always more effective together. Some of us are activists, some are lovers, some are encouragers, some are students of the Word, some are intercessors, some are compassionate, some are leaders. Wherever our individual personalities fit, there is a place for each and every one of us.

I remember hearing a speaker say, "If we both think the same, one of us isn't needed." In the body of Christ, we each bring something different to the table. If we were all identical, someone wouldn't be needed.

Spiritual Gifts

It is within this framework of the body of Christ that what is known as "spiritual gifts" comes into play. All of us are given spiritual gifts that usually add to and enhance our basic personality strength, unless the Lord calls us to a ministry for which we do not naturally have abilities. Then He gives us a special gift needed to perform the tasks at hand.

The theology of spiritual gifts is vast and controversial. One could spend months studying it. For our purposes here, we are going to take a middle-of-the-road approach, since my desire is to show how your spiritual personality and your spiritual gift connect. You already understand personalities. Now let's get a quick overview of spiritual gifts.

If you are not familiar with the general body of teaching known as spiritual gifts, let me give you the definition that most clearly applies to our study of personalities and spiritual gifts. The New Unger's Bible Dictionary says *spiritual gift* means "any extraordinary faculty, which operated for the furtherance of the welfare of the Christian community, and which was itself wrought by the grace of God, through the power of the Holy Spirit, in special individuals, in accordance, respectively, with the measure of their individual capacities, whether it were that the Spirit infused entirely new powers, or stimulated those already existing to higher power and activity."

There are four major Bible passages from which teaching on spiritual gifts is derived. The first we explore is Romans 12:3–8:

> Because God has given me a special gift, I have something to say to *everyone* among you. Do not think you are better than you are. You must decide what you really are by the amount of faith God has given you. *Each* one of us has a body with many parts, and these parts all have different uses. In the same way, we are many, but in Christ we are all one body. *Each* one is a part of that body, and each part belongs to all the other parts. We *all* have different gifts, each of which came because of the grace God gave us. The person who has the gift of prophecy should use that gift in agreement with the faith. Anyone who has the gift of serving should serve. Anyone who has the gift of teaching should teach. Whoever has the gift of encouraging others should encourage. Whoever has the gift of giving to others should give freely. Anyone who has the gift of being a leader should try hard when he leads. Whoever has the gift of showing mercy to others should do so with joy [Romans 12:3–8 NCV].

As you read those verses, be sure to note the inclusiveness. We all have a gift. I have placed key words in italics to help you see that clearly.

Next, we review 1 Corinthians 12 (specifically verses 1, 4–11, and 28–30):

> Now, brothers and sisters, I want you to understand about spiritual gifts. . . .
>
> There are different kinds of gifts, but they are all from the same Spirit. There are different ways to serve but the same Lord to serve. And there are different ways that God works through people but the same God. God works in all of us in everything we do. Something from the Spirit can be seen in each person, for the common good. The Spirit gives one person the ability to *speak with wisdom*, and the same Spirit gives another the ability to *speak with knowledge*. The same Spirit gives *faith* to one person. And, to another, that one Spirit gives gifts of healing. The Spirit gives to another person the power to do miracles, to another the ability to prophesy. And he gives to another the *ability to know the difference between good and evil spirits*. The Spirit gives one person the ability to speak in different kinds of languages and to another the ability to interpret those languages. One Spirit, the same Spirit, does all these things, and the Spirit decides what to give each person. . . .
>
> In the church God has given a place first to apostles, second to prophets, and third to teachers. Then God has given a place to those who do miracles, those who have gifts of healing, those who can *help* others, those who are able to *govern*, and those who can speak in different languages. Not all are apostles. Not all are prophets. Not all are teachers. Not all do miracles. Not all have gifts of healing. Not all speak in different languages. Not all interpret those languages [1 Corinthians 12:1–30 NCV].

In the Corinthians passage, we see an emphasis on the differences in the various spiritual gifts (italics added). Next, notice the focus on unity found in the section of Scripture from Ephesians 4, especially verses 3–6 and 11–12:

> You are joined together with peace through the Spirit, so make every effort to continue together in this way. There is one body and

one Spirit, and God called you to have one hope. There is one Lord, one faith, and one baptism. There is one God and Father of everything. He rules everything and is everywhere and is in everything. Christ gave *each* one of us the special gift of grace, showing how generous he is. That is why it says in the Scriptures, "When he went up to the heights, he led a parade of captives, and he gave gifts to people. . . ."

And Christ gave gifts to people—he made some to be apostles, some to be *prophets*, some *to go and tell the Good News*, and some to have the work of *caring for and teaching God's people*. Christ gave those gifts to prepare God's holy people for the work of serving, to make the body of Christ stronger [Ephesians 4:3–12, NCV].

The last passage is 1 Peter 4. As you read these selected verses, notice the repetition of the idea that these gifts are for everyone, and pay attention to *why* we receive these gifts.

Each of you has received a gift to use to serve others. Be good servants of God's various gifts of grace. Anyone who *speaks* should speak words from God. Anyone who *serves* should serve with the strength God gives so that in everything God will be praised through Jesus Christ. Power and glory belong to him forever and ever. Amen [1 Peter 4:10–11, NCV].

The verses from Peter mention only two gifts; interestingly, all of the other gifts fit within one of those two gifts, allowing them to serve as major groupings. Note that there is some controversy as to which of the gifts mentioned in these scriptures are for us today; various teachings on the topic list seven, fourteen, or more gifts. Because my goal here is to show the connection to your spiritual personality and your spiritual gifts—rather than to write the end-all treatise on the topic—I am avoiding the controversy. The gifts I am using are italicized to make it easier for you to follow. I am grateful that my friend Judy Wallace allowed me to benefit from her original research on the topic as I shared with her my information on the personalities. She has done a more in-depth study that can be found in her book *In His Presents* (Baptist Publishing House, 2002).

To look at how spiritual gifts connect, let's first divide the gifts in these passages into the two groups from the passage in Peter. Because I have chosen to use a contemporary version of the Bible, I am also listing the more traditional term associated with each gift.

Speaking

Prophecy	Prophet
Tell the Good News	Evangelist
Caring for and teaching	Pastor-teacher
Speak with wisdom	Word of wisdom
Leader	Leadership
Able to govern	Administration

Serving

Serving	Server
Help others	Helps
Show mercy	Mercy
Giving	Giving
Ability to know the difference	Discernment
Faith	Faith
Speak with knowledge	Knowledge
Encouraging others	Exhortation

The groupings indicated—speaking and serving—should remind you of the personalities. When we look at the chart of four squares from Chapter One, we see that the top two personalities (Popular Sanguine and Powerful Choleric) are more of the speakers, and the bottom two (Peaceful Phlegmatic and Perfect Melancholy) more of the servers. But if we look at a definition of each gift, we see the connection is a bit more complicated.

From her research, Judy Wallace divides these groupings one more time, to four. She calls them Public Proclaimers, Prepared Planners, Private Performers, and Profound Perceivers.

The gifts in the Public Proclaimers group are those who are out front teaching, instructing, inspiring, guiding, and witnessing. This group is made up of Prophet, Evangelist, Pastor-Teacher, and Word of Wisdom. Let's look closer at each of these gifts. As you read each description (modified here from her work), think of the personalities.

• Prophet: the Prophet is truth-oriented. These are people who can quickly assess a situation and then speak up to confront a wrong. They have public boldness and do not mind calling a kettle black whenever and wherever necessary. In a church setting, those with a gift of prophecy often stay quiet for fear of being misunderstood or resented. Prophets generally feel that what they have to say is too harsh. But the church needs prophets. They are the people who keep us in line and will do so in a way that is honoring to God.

• Evangelist: the Evangelist is soul-oriented. These people have a deep, constant burden for the lost. All Christians are meant to be soul winners, but it comes easily to the Evangelists. They have a burning desire to see people brought to the saving knowledge of Christ. They can usually turn any situation into a witnessing opportunity.

• Teacher: the Teacher is concept-oriented. Those with the gift of teaching have the ability to discover and analyze the truth of God's Word and then share its concepts with others in a way they can truly understand. They enjoy studying the Scriptures, researching each passage, and then delivering the message simply, clearly, and accurately.

• Word of Wisdom: those with the Word of Wisdom gift are application-oriented. They do not just want to know the concepts of the Bible; they want us to be able to apply them to our own daily life. They teach, preach, and write in such a way as to help us practice what we preach. These people are practical in their presentation and give us practical ways of following what they have taught.

The gifts in the Prepared Planners group are those who see what needs to be done, make the plans, and then motivate the troops to accomplish those plans. They are the big-picture people, envisioning the end result and organizing all it takes to get there. This group includes Leadership and Administration.

- Leadership: these people are goal-oriented. They assume responsibility and leadership. They know what resources are needed and available to reach the goals. This role brings with it both responsibility and accountability. People in this position need to realize they are easy targets for criticism. Leaders often seem insensitive when delegating and need to remember the church is a group of people with God-given ministries, not a to-do list.
- Administration: these people are task-oriented. They are self-starters and take care of the details necessary to reach the goal. They help implement and execute the ideas and plans of the leader.

The gifts in the Private Performers group are the ones that get things done. They accomplish the job without taking any part of the limelight. The gifts in this category are Service, Helps, Mercy, and Giving.

- Service: those with the gift of service are needs-oriented. They assist or support people in a practical way, which gives them joy. Their satisfaction comes from ensuring that the ministry of the preceding two groups runs smoothly.
- Helps: people with the gift of helps are also needs-oriented, but instead of the focus being on helping people it is on taking care of things. They are concerned with the logistics of the service or activity. They do not care if they are noticed; they just want to help and know that what they are doing needs to be done.

• Mercy: those with the gift of mercy are feelings-oriented. They show more than sympathy; they have empathy. Sympathy feels for others; empathy feels with others. They are concerned with the person. When others are sad, they cry with them. When others are happy, they laugh with them. They do both sincerely. They give warmth, hope, and comfort to those around them.

• Giving: these people are cause-oriented. They usually, but not always, have the capacity to make money and then find true joy in giving to help others. We all give, but these people go above and beyond. If there is a financial need, they fill it. If someone needs food, clothes, or transportation, these people see to it that they have it. Not always do the givers have an abundance of means. They are never afraid, however, to share what they have with others. The key to this gift is that it is all usually done in secret. They do not give for show; they have no hidden motives. They simply enjoy meeting the material needs of people and organizations.

The Profound Perceivers observe others and their actions and seem to have an insight as to their motives. They help fine-tune activities. This group includes Discernment, Faith, Word of Knowledge, and Exhortation.

• Discernment: those with the gift of discernment can clearly distinguish between truth and error. They can detect false teachers and are usually the ones to see God's will and direction in spiritual matters. The church needs discerners to detect subtle errors and deficiencies in the truth.

• Faith: people who have the gift of faith have the ability to believe God above and beyond what is shown in the daily Christian walk—an extraordinary confidence in God's promises, power, and presence—so they can take heroic stands for their future and God's work in the church. Charles Swindoll describes it this way in *He Gave Gifts* (published by Insight for Living, 1992): "the ability to discern God's will, pursue it with extraordinary confidence and then lay hold of God's promises with remarkable results."

• Word of Knowledge: people with this gift find joy and motivation in study. They seek truth for themselves because they truly want to know what God is saying. They spend a lot of time in prayer and in God's Word digging for the truth. Others seek them out because of their greater understanding of what God is saying. Those with this gift encourage others in the Christian walk.

• Exhortation: people with this gift seek to motivate and support others, enabling them to move forward in their Christian life. They come alongside another to assist, help, or encourage. Those with this gift have the ability to see the steps of action that are necessary to lead others to maturity. They can visualize the potential spiritual achievement of people and will confront individuals when necessary to spur them toward the goal. They also have the ability to bring harmony between divergent parties.

OK. You have a basic understanding of spiritual gifts—at least as they apply to this study. And you already understand the personalities. Now, how do they connect?

Let's go back to the previous definition of spiritual gifts (I have italicized the key elements to which I want to draw your attention):

> Any extraordinary faculty, which operated for the furtherance of the welfare of the Christian community, and which was itself wrought by the grace of God, through the power of the Holy Spirit, in special individuals, in accordance, respectively, with the *measure of their individual capacities*, whether it were that the Spirit infused entirely new powers, *or stimulated those already existing to higher power and activity*.

(The phrase "entirely new powers" is going to get our attention later in this chapter.)

Regarding the portion in italics, notice that the spiritual gifts are in accordance with our individual capacity. Through the power of the Holy Spirit, our individual capacity is stimulated to higher power and activity. That means that for most of us, our spiritual gift and our personality—our individual capacity—are going to align. However, with the power of the Holy Spirit, our natural strengths will be stimulated to a higher power and activity.

Barbara found this to be true in her life. Her spiritual personality is primarily the Perfect Melancholy. She writes: "My Bible study and prayer times are very structured and consistent. From time to time, I vary my routine a little. This usually happens if I'm reading a book on prayer and learning something new, or a current group Bible study ends and I'm studying on my own. My structuring is also influenced by my spiritual gift of administration. My other main gift is teaching, which influences the types of books I read (very little 'fluff') and studies I pursue."

With this premise and the spiritual gifts, here is how I find they line up. First, we have the basic chart of the personalities. If we draw a diagonal line from the top left corner to the bottom right corner, it looks like the first figure shown here.

The personalities on the top of the diagonal line are the ones who naturally have what Peter calls the "Speaking" gifts; there is a high percentage of the Popular Sanguine, Powerful Choleric, or Perfect Melancholy. Likewise, those below the diagonal are most likely to have the gifts of "Serving."

If we place the listing of all of the gifts in a grid, it looks like the next figure. To determine which gifts are "in accordance with our individual capacities," we rotate the grid forty-five degrees, to match the diagonal line, as seen in the third figure.

With this assessment, those who have the Public Proclaimer gifts are a higher percentage of either the Popular Sanguine or the Powerful Choleric. Those who have the Prepared Planner gifts are either Powerful Choleric or Perfect Melancholy, and so on. For me, I am about fifty-fifty Popular Sanguine/Powerful Choleric. Naturally, I do not therefore have gifts in the Private Performer grouping.

Raelene's spiritual gift aligns with her Powerful Choleric/Popular Sanguine. She recently told me that she most enjoys working in her gift of Administration. She also shared that people constantly tease her about the way she organizes everything. She admits, "I need to

function efficiently—from my cupboards to my craft room and my office. Even my calendar is organized with color-coded entries."

Raelene shared this story: "This is my third year working on the committee of a regional women's conference. I am in charge of ticket sales. The 'teasing' from within the group concerns my charts. Records are needed for flow and tracking purposes. I love creating thorough charts—probably offering more information than others care for. But this is where my spiritual personality works best—having fun creating and at the same time, accomplishing the details of organizing the sales of two thousand to five thousand tickets."

She continues, "I've often thought that if I ever wanted to do any other job on the committee, the rest of the group wouldn't let

Public Proclaimers	Prepared Planners
Prophet Evangelist Teacher or Pastor Word of wisdom	Leadership Administration
Profound Perceivers Discernment Faith Word of knowledge Exhortation	Private Performers Service Helps Mercy Giving

me—they have too much fun 'teasing' me . . . and trusting me. But that's OK, I really do love what I do."

In our Chapter Six, Peter shared how he loves to study, but found that few people wanted to hear about all he has learned. As a Perfect Melancholy, his spiritual gifting ties in perfectly with his personality. Peter writes, "God has given me a ministry to young men. I mentor them one-on-one, developing a vision and timeline for their life and destiny in God. I am able to incorporate my knowledge and my spiritual gift of service. It provides me with great joy to assist these young men in such a practical way."

Notice I said "naturally." This brings us to the second aspect of understanding how our personality and spiritual gifts connect. The elements of the definition I underlined come into play here. The Holy Spirit can infuse entirely new powers, gifts that are not natural to our personality.

In the previous chapter, we looked at the body of Christ being the church and how, as the group comes together, all of the personality strengths are present. Still, if God calls us to a work, either individually or corporately, where the needed skills are not present,

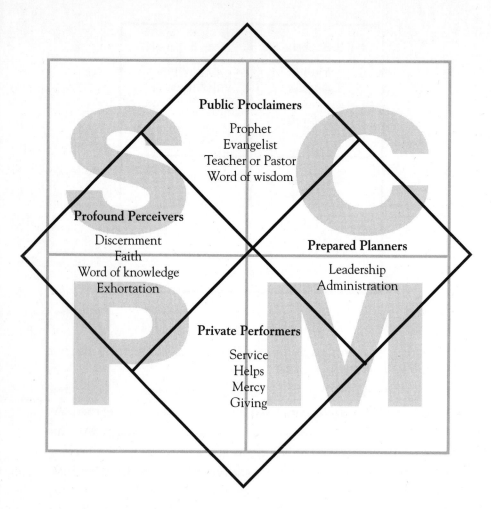

He supernaturally bestows us with a spiritual gift to accomplish the task at hand—"extraordinary faculty, . . . for the furtherance of the welfare of the Christian community." In his best-selling book *Purpose Driven Life* (Zondervan, 2002), Rick Warren affirms this by saying, "Whenever God gives us an assignment, He always equips us with what we need to accomplish it" (p. 236).

My mother's personality is very much like mine. Her spiritual gifts are all in the two areas you would expect for a Popular Sanguine/

Powerful Choleric: Public Proclaimers and Prepared Planners. Her spiritual gifts are prophet, teacher, word of wisdom, leader. I remember many years ago when both of us took a spiritual gifts inventory. In the mercy category, we each scored in the minus range. Yet, while my father was alive, God called my mom to minister beside him in his work to those who had suffered abuse, especially sexual abuse. Her natural self would want to run from these people and their sad stories, but God gave her a special gift of mercy that allowed her to give warmth, hope, and comfort to others. Since my father's death, that is no longer a part of her life, and today she functions primarily in areas of her gifting.

Like my mother's, Van's personality would preclude her having gifts in the Private Performer grouping—unless God specifically calls her to a ministry where those gifts are needed, which is the case for Van. She shares: "I am a typical Popular Sanguine/Powerful Choleric with the gift of teaching as my primary gift. It gives me great joy and I am filled with all the energy I need when I stand before a group. It can be high school teenagers in a public school classroom, ladies in a Bible study or a women's celebration at a banquet."

What Van has noticed is that God has also blessed her with the gift of service so that she can minister to those at the events she leads. She says, "At this stage in my life I teach Bible and parenting classes to ladies at the Pregnancy Care Center in my community. These women are most often in a state of crisis when they arrive. They are overwhelmed with the fact that they are in the midst of an unplanned pregnancy and they have no one to whom they can turn for emotional support or financial assistance."

In Van's case, she reports that the circumstances are even more overwhelming because the young women she sees are Latinas. They are in a foreign and strange place, do not speak the language, and have no family. She admits, "It is truly an unhappy situation, one that is very far from my comfort zone."

Van continues: "Unplanned pregnancies have placed these women in compromising circumstances. They are facing poverty. The men in their lives are abusive. They have no money for their immediate medical needs. But God . . . has given me such compassion and love for these women and equipped me to serve them."

There's an old saying that goes, "They don't care how much you know, until they know how much you care." Armed with that understanding, Van declares, "I can speak their language, many are teenagers, and, because they have chosen to keep their babies, I admire them and want to help. I can reach these ladies for Christ because He has called me to teach with a positive upbeat flavor and to serve with a kind, open, and hope-filled presence." Van has learned that without the ability to serve them, all the lessons on parenting or Bible-centered classes would fall on deaf ears if they weren't recipients of tangible needs that proved to them that she cares.

Sharen's personality and natural giftings are different from my mother's and Van's, but she too has found that God has equipped her specially for His service. She says that as she matures in Christ, her gifts sometimes shift to something other than her natural personality. As a Popular Sanguine/Peaceful Phlegmatic, Sharen says:

> I don't think my natural bent would be to organize and run a Writer's Guild, but it's only by God's grace and His will in my life. I could not do it without Him. . . . I know that for a *fact!* I'm so glad He offers the gifts we need when *He* needs them. He is amazing! When we surrender ourselves to Him, He moves in miraculous ways through anyone He wants, regardless of our natural personality. But, I know He also makes it easier on us too, to work in harmony with the personalities He created in us. Either way, His will be done for His glory!

Our personality and our spiritual gifts do connect. The two together give you your vision and purpose—a reason to get out of bed every day and serve God. They keep us on track. Once we claim our strengths, we are ready to move into service. "Strength is for service, not status. Each one of us needs to look after the good of the people around us, asking ourselves, 'How can I help?' That's exactly what Jesus did" (Romans 15:1–2, MSG).

Lecia found this combination of knowledge was powerful in her life. She writes, "Since learning about the personalities in August of 2002 I no longer question who I am, I *understand* who I am; by adding the knowledge of what I am gifted to do God has given me an even greater understanding. By bringing the two together (personality and spiritual gifting) I can understand who God created me to be, and what He's created me to do." She knows that it still takes following His will, and seeking His guidance daily; but this knowledge keeps her on track for what He's created her for.

Remember, each of us has a spiritual gift. Many of us may have several. Just like our individual personality, no one gift is better or more important than any other. God gave us gifts so that we can further the welfare of the Christian community, so we can contribute to the wider good of the church. Our personality is our natural state. The King James Version of the Ephesians passage says, "For the perfecting of the saints, for the work of the ministry, for the edifying of the body of Christ" (Ephesians 4:12, KJV). Our spiritual gifts perfect us. Or, as the Living Bible says, "Why is it that he gives us these special abilities to do certain things best? It is that God's people will be equipped to do better work for him, building up the Church, the body of Christ, to a position of strength and maturity" (Ephesians 4:12, TLB). My purpose here is to guide you in claiming your natural personality and in perfecting it, to bring you to a "position of strength and maturity" in Him.

Chapter Ten

Encouragement and Freedom

When you have a right-standing relationship with
God, you have a life of freedom, liberty and
delight; you are God's will.
  —*Oswald Chambers*, My Utmost for His Highest

One of the great joys of understanding your spiritual personality is the encouragement and freedom it gives you and allows you to give to others. I hope that as you read these pages you have found both encouragement and freedom—encouragement in who you are and freedom to develop your relationship with God.

I hope that, as with Barbara, it has strengthened you to know that you are not alone. Barbara has been encouraged to read that she is not so very different from other Perfect Melancholies when it comes to her quiet time.

Jeanne has been encouraged as well, and it has helped her to know that her struggles are not due to her faultiness, lack of commitment, or knowledge deficit; the feelings she's had are shared by many others and are normal for who God made us to be. Knowing this helps her to be at peace with it and relax. Jeanne told me, "I can accept that God loves me for who I am, that I don't have to get it perfect for Him—but He understands why I try so hard."

Most importantly, I hope that you have gained a new freedom in your relationship with God. After all, that is the wonderful quality that the Christian life offers us. So much of the New Testament is about freedom. Perhaps the best-known verse addressing our freedom in Christ is John 8:36: "Therefore if the Son makes you free, you shall be free indeed" (NKJV). 2 Corinthians 3:17 is another that affirms this privilege: "Now the Lord is the Spirit, and where the Spirit of the Lord is, there is freedom" (NIV). But my personal favorite is Romans 7:6: "But now that we're no longer shackled to that domineering mate of sin, and out from under all those oppressive regulations and fine print, we're free to live a new life in the freedom of God" (MSG).

Doesn't it amaze you that when God so wants us to have freedom, people continuously want to give others rules in their relationship with God? Fortunately, Ruth discovered the freedom of God before her world fell apart recently. She shared with me that she is fifty-three and was raised in a church that not only taught the Gospel but also outlined the habits and behavior of the "saintly" saint. The men wore suits with shirts and ties, while the women wore black, brown, or navy dresses that covered them from neck to ankle. They were to read the Bible every day and pray for a minimum amount of time each day, and *every time* the doors were open for service they were in church. They were not allowed to go anywhere that the "world" went, which meant no movies, bowling, baseball games, and so on. In hindsight, Ruth says, "I always found it odd that I could go sledding with my friends." The tightness of these requirements gradually eased with the passing of the generations, but the guilt of not doing them persisted.

While in her teens, she joined another church. This new church taught the Gospel, although it taught a different set of habits and behavior, which included being able to do anything you wanted as long as you were a Christian.

Later she joined another church that tried a middle-of-the-road approach with requirements that included daily Bible reading and minimum prayer along with weekly attendance at two to three services. The dress code was more flexible, but not relaxed since you were expected to dress as though you expected at any moment to meet the president of the United States of America.

Through all of this, Ruth tried to follow the rules, whether they were spoken or not, yet felt she never managed to do it right all the time. She worked at being perfect, so she would be more like

Christ, and to win the approval of others, but when trouble came into her life, she would go into an emotional tailspin. She said, "I felt I could not go to God for help since I had 'failed' to keep the spiritual to-do list." When she came to a major crisis point later in her life, this thinking left her feeling so alone and unloved by God that her life nearly came to an untimely end.

It was in the midst of this struggle that Ruth first began to understand her spiritual personality. She was already familiar with the personalities from earlier study, but by understanding the *spiritual* personality she was released to start relating to God the way He created her.

Ruth says she still likes to read and study God's word, but some days she just reads a verse, or recites a verse that comes to her mind. Instead of a set length of time in her prayer closet, she prays throughout the day, and she dresses modestly with color and comfort in mind. She now enjoys her relationship with the Lord, and when trouble comes she goes right to Him, knowing that He loves her unconditionally.

Ruth's personal world was thrown into total upheaval a couple of months ago, but she has peace like never before. She said she feels as "snug as a bug in a rug" in the arms of her heavenly Father, and she looks at this time in her life as the greatest opportunity ever to see Him do marvelous things in and through her. She is living the abundant life in the midst of a tremendous storm, and she knows that understanding her spiritual personality has played a significant part in getting to this place in her relationship with the Lord. In addition, Ruth feels it has helped her to be gracious to those who have played the adversary role during this time because she realizes part of the problem is the difference in our spiritual personalities. She declared, "I have never felt so free!"

As I reviewed the responses that formed the basis for this book, read e-mails sent in response, and talked to people after speaking on this topic, I found that, as happened for Ruth, a sense of release to be who God made us each to be is probably the greatest benefit of understanding our spiritual personality.

Lecia shared her reactions with me. When she began to under-stand her spiritual personality, it opened up a whole new world of understanding of herself, her walk as a Christian, and her family. In the past, there were times she thought she was crazy. Not crazy like jump off a rooftop, but crazy like, "Why do I think like this? Why does this stuff (whatever it is) bother me so much?" She remembers exclaiming "Oh, that's me! Now it makes sense!" Now she can see that "*it all makes sense.*"

Gloria was in a "spiritual comparison trap," and understanding her spiritual personality is what released her from that. Before she understood her spiritual personality, she believed the lie that her fun nature and loud personality prohibited her from getting as close to God as her more serious friends. She states, "Now I have a much closer walk with the Lord knowing that I can laugh and come to God just as He created me." This understanding also granted her permission to use the wonderful, zany personality traits that the Lord gave her, not only to live out her Christian life but to study and worship Him without guilt or questioning about her approach.

Ruth has found her relationship with God has grown. She relates that as she has grown in the understanding of her spiritual personality, she has also grown more balanced in her thinking both about God and herself. She realizes that when God first thought of her, He put this wonderful personality mix in her along with so many other fascinating things that make up who she is. Under-standing this has given her a tremendous boost in her relationship with the Lord. Ruth says, "It has taken me a while to understand my personality, but it is a great tool for spiritual growth."

Once you have accepted who God made you to be and are basking in that liberty, I hope you will have a closer walk with the Lord and that you will desire to know Him in deeper and richer ways. Experiment with what works for you as you grow closer to Him. Start by trying the things listed for your spiritual personality, the things that have worked for others like you. But then, branch out. Try the techniques and worship styles of the other personali-ties. You may find some that work for you.

As a constantly moving-and-doing Popular Sanguine/Powerful Choleric, I see that my relationship with God takes on this same quality. But when I am able, I find that I feel closest to God alone on a rock in the wilderness. I practically become contemplative when I am surrounded by nature without another human being in sight. My life seldom allows this luxury, but it adds another dimension to my relationship with God. When I am still, I breathe deeply and know that He is God.

You'll never know which of the various ways in which people grow closer to God will work for you until you try them. Fran shares my same personality mix. She tried something outside of her natural personality and found it did not work for her; contemplative prayer was too restricting and too quiet. It requires sitting for thirty minutes, getting up and walking in a circle for five minutes, then sitting again for thirty minutes, and repeating that for a whole day. After the first fifteen minutes, she says, her legs would start wiggling up and down and it took all she had to contain herself and sit still until she could jump up for the five minutes of walking. Although Fran knows contemplative prayer is not for her, it was a good try.

So, don't rest in who you are. I want to challenge you to first experience God through the person He made you to be. Then, once you have developed a style or system that works for you, move beyond your comfort zone and try new things that can add depth and richness to your spiritual personality. Just as we do not want to be stuck in a box, we want to grow and mature to become more like Christ, so you will want to expand your spiritual life.

Almost everything we have discussed in this book is to help you grow in your relationship with God, but it's not all about you. It is about your family, your friends, and the people with whom you go to church. With an understanding of spiritual personalities, you can effectively encourage others in their Christian walk and give them the freedom to grow and worship as God made them.

You met Laurie in Chapters Three, Four, and Seven. Understanding her spiritual personality has helped her learn to enjoy God. But it has also allowed her to set others free from judgment.

As she learned about the spiritual personalities, the nagging feelings of not doing things right spiritually began to dissipate. These feelings were replaced by a hunger and a curiosity that perhaps God had created her *intentionally* to be who she was, spiritually speaking. This didn't mean giving herself permission to be lazy in her walk with Him, without a thought of working at it. Rather, she discovered that God smiles at her unconventional ways of enjoying Him. The more she enjoys Him, the more she wants to work at getting closer to Him. Understanding this has literally changed Laurie's walk with God.

Laurie reminds us in Matthew 22:37 and 38 (NIV) that Jesus gave us a pretty simple and straightforward commandment: "Love the Lord your God with all your heart and with all your soul and with all your mind. This is the first and greatest commandment." Learning our spiritual personality is a journey toward loving our God more fully. But then in verses 39 and 40, Jesus lets us know that this second commandment is just as important. "And the second is like it: 'Love your neighbor as yourself.' All the Law and the Prophets hang on these two commandments." Laurie says that our understanding the spiritual personalities is an invaluable tool in learning to love our neighbors, *even if they don't do it the way you think they should.* Once we learn how our own personality thrives, we also discover how the other three personalities flourish . . . and the judging stops there. Laurie always felt people were judging her and her unconventional ways. She told me, "I felt insecure with myself. Having this new knowledge gives me the confidence I need to move and act in the way God created me. And if people judge me, then I will give them this book!"

The wife of Marie's pastor appeared to be a wallflower next to her Powerful Choleric husband. But as Marie got to know her on a mission trip where they roomed together, Marie was able to help her blossom. Marie told me that her pastor is 100 percent-plus Powerful Choleric, and his wife nearly pure Perfect Melancholy. Each Sunday he would tell the church that he had a lot to do and would accomplish it with or without them. Week after week, he called on them to muster, but they never heard from his demure, seemingly dutiful, wife, who would sit quietly in the first row week after week.

Marie often wondered why her church never got to hear from the pastor's wife. Little did she know the pastor's wife would have been petrified to be the center of attention, and that she functioned well in her silent space.

Her pastor had a lot for the church to accomplish, but Marie's heart always steered toward his wife. She would often wonder, *What's wrong with her? Doesn't she love us or care?*

That was before Marie and the pastor's wife went to Guatemala together for a short-term mission. She really got to know her after living with her day after day. Marie learned this lady was a strong woman with a deep faith in God, and much of her husband's ministry rested on her ordered, methodical approach to matters. Marie also learned the reason the church had not heard from the pastor's wife was because she felt she was a failure to the flock and hid from them in despair. Not a dynamic personality or speaker, she had also mistakenly thought she was a disappointment.

Marie helped her pastor's wife identify her personality and her strengths, and encouraged her. This allowed her to come into a place of acceptance of who she was spiritually, and in the following months the church thought they had gotten a new pastor's wife. As she embraced who she was spiritually, she was able to reach out to others in the church. She changed even more when it was returned with love and acceptance from the congregation. In fact, she became so loved and revered, Marie said, "We even teased her that she was turning into a Popular Sanguine—in fact, she is becoming more like Christ."

Marie's pastor still marches them on and sets the bar high, but they are all marching toward the goals together. The difference is at their side they now have a solid, reliable woman of faith.

Do you know someone like Marie's pastor's wife? Someone who feels she does not measure up simply because she does not fit a preconceived mold of who she thinks she is supposed to be? Wouldn't it be great to see her set free? You can encourage her to be the person God made her to be as she begins to understand her spiritual personality.

Fortunately, Marie was able to spend time with her pastor's wife and encourage her. Chances are there were other people in the church who judged her. Probably at some point someone made her feel that who she was was wrong. It is human nature to think that someone different from us or from our preconceived ideas is wrong. But as you have learned, that is not the case.

Understanding and implementing the basic concepts of the spiritual personalities helps you maximize your relationship with God and others. Although it is a simple tool, it can make a big difference. Renee was part of a ministry team for five years, but she was deeply wounded by her pastor. Both had a basic understanding of the personalities—but failed to apply it in their relationship.

For five years one of Renee's friends was also her pastor, and a strong Powerful Choleric. In the beginning they worked together and enjoyed their friendship; however, the longer they continued the more they were in conflict. Often Renee heard statements from her pastor the likes of "You're bucking my authority!" "Don't be so perfectionistic." "You're Melancholy and there's a black cloud over your head." Renee's response to those comments was usually "Stop trying to control me!" Even with a basic understanding of the personalities, Renee recognized these were classic Choleric statements. Unfortunately, this situation ended with them both deeply hurt. Renee finally left the church resentful and depressed.

In the past two years, Renee's job has allowed her the opportunity to extensively study and develop training for manager classes based on the personalities materials. She now realizes just how sad this situation really was and that some of the conflict could have been avoided. While reading and listening to the personalities materials, she would often sit in her office crying: "Wow, I wish I'd known all this a couple of years before. It would have saved a lot of anxiety, stress and time—and possibly a friendship."

Renee and her pastor understood the personalities, but they failed to apply them to their personal conflict. Cathy, by contrast, has successfully applied her knowledge to the groups she leads as a Bible study teacher. She says: "Understanding the spiritual personalities has helped me be more Christ-like in my relationships. It opened my eyes as to what my weaknesses are, enabling me to give more grace to others when they get on my nerves with behaviors that are not like mine."

Cathy's Bible study groups, like most groups, have comprised a mixture of the spiritual personalities. Learning the spiritual personalities has helped her structure the two-hour group time so that all the personalities' needs are met. As an example, for the Popular Sanguines she plans a time for socialization during the first fifteen minutes and then after the study. For those Perfect Melancholies, the Bible study time is pretty structured, with a study book to follow. The study book questions can be completed prior to meeting, answered, and shared at the meeting—but it is not required. The choice is each person's whether to do the week's study prior to meeting and then share with the group, or just answer the questions during group time. Choices are there, so that everyone is happy. Personal sharing is encouraged, but when someone (usually the Popular Sanguine) gets too far off the trail, the Perfect Melancholy is assigned the bunny ears (like a peace sign), to let the person know he's on a "rabbit trail" and pull him back to the present.

Cathy understands that a Bible study group with members all of one personality could get pretty boring. She has learned that we need to please all of the personalities in one way or another. Studying the personalities has helped her realize this and given her ways to try to make it happen. Cathy states that "a big part of having a well-rounded group is accepting others as they are."

Christ accepted each of us, with all of our differences. We did not have to get our act together before we came to Christ. We can offer others that same freedom. Ruth recently told me that her understanding of the spiritual personalities has strengthened her relationships with family and friends. She shares that her son appreciates how she has also stopped being the spiritual watchdog with others and has started enjoying and celebrating the differences.

It is easy for parents to believe they know what is best for their child, and parents should of course steer their child's spiritual life. But if your child is a different personality from you—and you do not understand the concept of the spiritual personalities—you could be doing more harm than good. My friend Georgia found that her son, a Popular Sanguine, was rebelling against his mother's religion because he watched her faith expressed in her Perfect Melancholy way. It did not seem to be any fun to him. The structure and discipline was comfortable for her, but not for him.

Pamela has a similar concern for her children. She shared with me that it is her desire for her children to have a personal relationship with Jesus Christ, and that she is able to provide a home that fully promotes this. With a mother's heart, she frets that her son and daughter may not be growing in their faith as sincerely as they should. However, once she learned about the spiritual personalities, she could see how her children are indeed personally relating to God, each in their own way—very real and personal. Pamela says, "I am thankful for having a tool that helps me to better see the truth in my precious children."

Georgia and Pamela are both Perfect Melancholy. Raelene is more Choleric, yet she faced a similar fear with her eighteen-year-old son, Aaron, that was alleviated by an understanding of the personalities.

Aaron is a gentle, creative musician and writer, as well as a contemplative kid (Peaceful Phlegmatic/Perfect Melancholy). Raelene admits that she is constantly asking him if he's OK. He always says he is, but it's hard for her to get it. According to her personality (Powerful Choleric with some Popular Sanguine), she thinks "OK" means happy, lively, and talkative. Raelene is quite talkative, and when she tells a story she wants to know and give all the details—unlike Aaron's conversation style, which is brief, addressing just what anyone needs to know. When it comes to studying the Word, he wants the overview, without all the details.

Raelene became concerned when Aaron began asking her less and less about God and the Bible. She worried that he was "leaving his faith." It turns out that he just wanted basic answers to his questions, while she was pulling out every resource she had to give him the "full" answer. Now she knows that if she wants to have godly conversation with her son, she must keep it simple.

So this book is about your relationship with God, friends, family, and church members and how they work with your God-created personality. You are God's will. His desire is that you will be an expression of Him. Embrace your spiritual personality. Use it as a tool for growth. Encourage others in their individual Christian walk. Putting this into practice gives you encouragement and freedom— encouragement to be who you are and freedom to develop your relationship with God.

From today on, feel the freedom to be yourself. As you fulfill that purpose and do His will, you will ultimately bring glory to Him.

Personality Testing Instrument

Your Personality Profile

Directions: In each of the following rows of four words across, place an X in front of the word that most often applies to you. Continue through all forty lines. If you are not sure which word "most applies," ask a spouse or a friend, and think of what your answer would have been when you were a child. Use the word definitions in Appendix B for the most accurate results.

STRENGTHS

1	☐ Adventurous	☐ Adaptable	☐ Animated	☐ Analytical
2	☐ Persistent	☐ Playful	☐ Persuasive	☐ Peaceful
3	☐ Submissive	☐ Self-sacrificing	☐ Sociable	☐ Strong-willed
4	☐ Considerate	☐ Controlled	☐ Competitive	☐ Convincing
5	☐ Refreshing	☐ Respectful	☐ Reserved	☐ Resourceful
6	☐ Satisfied	☐ Sensitive	☐ Self-reliant	☐ Spirited
7	☐ Planner	☐ Patient	☐ Positive	☐ Promoter
8	☐ Sure	☐ Spontaneous	☐ Scheduled	☐ Shy
9	☐ Orderly	☐ Obliging	☐ Outspoken	☐ Optimistic
10	☐ Friendly	☐ Faithful	☐ Funny	☐ Forceful
11	☐ Daring	☐ Delightful	☐ Diplomatic	☐ Detailed
12	☐ Cheerful	☐ Consistent	☐ Cultured	☐ Confident
13	☐ Idealistic	☐ Independent	☐ Inoffensive	☐ Inspiring
14	☐ Demonstrative	☐ Decisive	☐ Dry humor	☐ Deep
15	☐ Mediator	☐ Musical	☐ Mover	☐ Mixes easily
16	☐ Thoughtful	☐ Tenacious	☐ Talker	☐ Tolerant

17	☐ Listener	☐ Loyal	☐ Leader	☐ Lively
18	☐ Contented	☐ Chief	☐ Chartmaker	☐ Cute
19	☐ Perfectionist	☐ Pleasant	☐ Productive	☐ Popular
20	☐ Bouncy	☐ Bold	☐ Behaved	☐ Balanced

WEAKNESSES

21	☐ Blank	☐ Bashful	☐ Brassy	☐ Bossy
22	☐ Undisciplined	☐ Unsympathetic	☐ Unenthusiastic	☐ Unforgiving
23	☐ Reticent	☐ Resentful	☐ Resistant	☐ Repetitious
24	☐ Fussy	☐ Fearful	☐ Forgetful	☐ Frank
25	☐ Impatient	☐ Insecure	☐ Indecisive	☐ Interrupts
26	☐ Unpopular	☐ Uninvolved	☐ Unpredictable	☐ Unaffectionate
27	☐ Headstrong	☐ Haphazard	☐ Hard to please	☐ Hesitant
28	☐ Plain	☐ Pessimistic	☐ Proud	☐ Permissive
29	☐ Angered easily	☐ Aimless	☐ Argumentative	☐ Alienated
30	☐ Naive	☐ Negative attitude	☐ Nervy	☐ Nonchalant
31	☐ Worrier	☐ Withdrawn	☐ Workaholic	☐ Wants credit
32	☐ Too sensitive	☐ Tactless	☐ Timid	☐ Talkative
33	☐ Doubtful	☐ Disorganized	☐ Domineering	☐ Depressed
34	☐ Inconsistent	☐ Introvert	☐ Intolerant	☐ Indifferent
35	☐ Messy	☐ Moody	☐ Mumbles	☐ Manipulative
36	☐ Slow	☐ Stubborn	☐ Show-off	☐ Skeptical
37	☐ Loner	☐ Lord over others	☐ Lazy	☐ Loud
38	☐ Sluggish	☐ Suspicious	☐ Short-tempered	☐ Scatterbrained
39	☐ Revengeful	☐ Restless	☐ Reluctant	☐ Rash
40	☐ Compromising	☐ Critical	☐ Crafty	☐ Changeable

Personality Scoring Sheet

Now transfer all your Xs to the corresponding words on the Personality Scoring Sheet, and add up your totals. For example, if you checked Animated on the profile, check it on the scoring sheet. (Note: The words are in a different order on the profile and the scoring sheet.)

STRENGTHS

	Popular Sanguine	Powerful Choleric	Perfect Melancholy	Peaceful Phlegmatic
1	☐ Animated	☐ Adventurous	☐ Analytical	☐ Adaptable
2	☐ Playful	☐ Persuasive	☐ Persistent	☐ Peaceful
3	☐ Sociable	☐ Strong-willed	☐ Self-sacrificing	☐ Submissive
4	☐ Convincing	☐ Competitive	☐ Considerate	☐ Controlled
5	☐ Refreshing	☐ Resourceful	☐ Respectful	☐ Reserved
6	☐ Spirited	☐ Self-reliant	☐ Sensitive	☐ Satisfied
7	☐ Promoter	☐ Positive	☐ Planner	☐ Patient
8	☐ Spontaneous	☐ Sure	☐ Scheduled	☐ Shy
9	☐ Optimistic	☐ Outspoken	☐ Orderly	☐ Obliging
10	☐ Funny	☐ Forceful	☐ Faithful	☐ Friendly
11	☐ Delightful	☐ Daring	☐ Detailed	☐ Diplomatic
12	☐ Cheerful	☐ Confident	☐ Cultured	☐ Consistent
13	☐ Inspiring	☐ Independent	☐ Idealistic	☐ Inoffensive
14	☐ Demonstrative	☐ Decisive	☐ Deep	☐ Dry humor
15	☐ Mixes easily	☐ Mover	☐ Musical	☐ Mediator
16	☐ Talker	☐ Tenacious	☐ Thoughtful	☐ Tolerant
17	☐ Lively	☐ Leader	☐ Loyal	☐ Listener
18	☐ Cute	☐ Chief	☐ Chartmaker	☐ Contented
19	☐ Popular	☐ Productive	☐ Perfectionist	☐ Pleasant
20	☐ Bouncy	☐ Bold	☐ Behaved	☐ Balanced
Total Strengths	☐	☐	☐	☐

WEAKNESSES

	Popular Sanguine	Powerful Choleric	Perfect Melancholy	Peaceful Phlegmatic
21	☐ Brassy	☐ Bossy	☐ Bashful	☐ Blank
22	☐ Undisciplined	☐ Unsympathetic	☐ Unforgiving	☐ Unenthusiastic
23	☐ Repetitious	☐ Resistant	☐ Resentful	☐ Reticent
24	☐ Forgetful	☐ Frank	☐ Fussy	☐ Fearful
25	☐ Interrupts	☐ Impatient	☐ Insecure	☐ Indecisive

26	☐ Unpredictable	☐ Unaffectionate	☐ Unpopular	☐ Uninvolved
27	☐ Haphazard	☐ Headstrong	☐ Hard to please	☐ Hesitant
28	☐ Permissive	☐ Proud	☐ Pessimistic	☐ Plain
29	☐ Angered easily	☐ Argumentative	☐ Alienated	☐ Aimless
30	☐ Naive	☐ Nervy	☐ Negative attitude	☐ Nonchalant
31	☐ Wants credit	☐ Workaholic	☐ Withdrawn	☐ Worrier
32	☐ Talkative	☐ Tactless	☐ Too sensitive	☐ Timid
33	☐ Disorganized	☐ Domineering	☐ Depressed	☐ Doubtful
34	☐ Inconsistent	☐ Intolerant	☐ Introvert	☐ Indifferent
35	☐ Messy	☐ Manipulative	☐ Moody	☐ Mumbles
36	☐ Show-off	☐ Stubborn	☐ Skeptical	☐ Slow
37	☐ Loud	☐ Lord over others	☐ Loner	☐ Lazy
38	☐ Scatterbrained	☐ Short-tempered	☐ Suspicious	☐ Sluggish
39	☐ Restless	☐ Rash	☐ Revengeful	☐ Reluctant
40	☐ Changeable	☐ Crafty	☐ Critical	☐ Compromising

Total
Weaknesses ☐ ☐ ☐ ☐

Combined
Totals ☐ ☐ ☐ ☐

Once you've transferred your answers to the scoring sheet, added up your total number of answers in each of the four columns, and added your totals from both the strengths and weaknesses sections, you'll know your dominant personality type. You'll also know what combination you are. If, for example, your score is 35 in Powerful Choleric strengths and weaknesses, there's really little question. You're almost all Powerful Choleric. But if your score is, for example, 16 in Powerful Choleric, 14 in Perfect Melancholy, and 5 in each of the others, you're a Powerful Choleric with a strong Perfect Melancholy. You'll also, of course, know your least dominant type. As you read and work with the material in this book, you'll learn how to put your strengths to work for you, how to compensate for the weaknesses in your dominant type, and how to understand the strengths and weaknesses of other types.

Appendix B

Personality Profile Word Definitions

STRENGTHS

1 **Adventurous** Takes on new and daring enterprises with a determination to master them.

Adaptable Easily fits and is comfortable in any situation.

Animated Full of life, lively use of hand, arm, and face gestures.

Analytical Likes to examine the parts for their logical and proper relationships.

2 **Persistent** Sees one project through to its completion before starting another.

Playful Full of fun and good humor.

Persuasive Convinces through logic and fact rather than charm or power.

Peaceful Seems undisturbed and tranquil and retreats from any form of strife.

3 **Submissive** Easily accepts any other's point of view or desire with little need to assert his or her own opinion.

Self-sacrificing Willingly gives up the needs of his or her own personal being for the sake of, or to meet the needs of, others.

Sociable Sees being with others as an opportunity to be cute and entertaining rather than as a challenge or business opportunity.

Strong-willed Determined to have one's own way.

4 **Considerate** Has regard for the needs and feelings of others.

Controlled Has emotional feelings but rarely displays them.

Competitive Turns every situation, happening, or game into a contest and always plays to win!

Convincing　Can win you over to anything through the sheer charm of his or her personality.

5 Refreshing　Renews and stimulates or makes others feel good.
Respectful　Treats others with deference, honor, and esteem.
Reserved　Self-restrained in expression of emotion or enthusiasm.
Resourceful　Able to act quickly and effectively in virtually all situations.

6 Satisfied　Easily accepts any circumstance or situation.
Sensitive　Intensively cares about others and what happens.
Self-reliant　Can fully rely on his or her own capabilities, judgment, and resources.
Spirited　Full of life and excitement.

7 Planner　Prefers to work out a detailed arrangement beforehand, for the accomplishment of project or goal, and prefers involvement with the planning stages and the finished product rather than the carrying out of the task.
Patient　Unmoved by delay, remains calm and tolerant.
Positive　Knows it will turn out right if he or she is in charge.
Promoter　Urges or compels others to go along, join, or invest through the charm of his or her own personality.

8 Sure　Confident, rarely hesitates or wavers.
Spontaneous　Prefers all of life to be impulsive, unpremeditated activity, not restricted by plans.
Scheduled　Makes, and lives according to, a daily plan, dislikes the plan to be interrupted.
Shy　Quiet, doesn't easily instigate a conversation.

9 Orderly　Has a methodical, systematic arrangement of things.
Obliging　Accommodating, is quick to do it another's way.
Outspoken　Speaks frankly and without reserve.
Optimistic　Sunny disposition, convinces self and others that everything will turn out all right.

10 Friendly　A responder rather than an initiator, seldom starts a conversation.
Faithful　Consistently reliable, steadfast, loyal, and devoted sometimes beyond reason.

Funny   Has a sparkling sense of humor that can make virtually any story into a hilarious event.

Forceful   Has a commanding personality which others would hesitate to take a stand against.

11 Daring   Willing to take risks; fearless, bold.

Delightful   Upbeat and fun to be with.

Diplomatic   Deals with people tactfully, sensitively, and patiently.

Detailed   Does everything in proper order with a clear memory of all the things that happen.

12 Cheerful   Consistently in good spirits and promoting happiness in others.

Consistent   Stays emotionally on an even keel, responding as one might expect.

Cultured   Has interests involving both intellectual and artistic pursuits, such as theatre, symphony, ballet.

Confident   Self-assured and certain of own ability and success.

13 Idealistic   Visualizes things in their perfect form, and has a need to measure up to that standard him- or herself.

Independent Self-sufficient, self-supporting, self-confident and seems to have little need of help.

Inoffensive Never says or causes anything unpleasant or objectionable.

Inspiring   Encourages others to work, join, or be involved, and makes the whole thing fun.

14 Demonstrative Openly expresses emotion, especially affection, and doesn't hesitate to touch others while speaking to them.

Decisive   A person with quick, conclusive, judgment-making ability.

Dry humor   Exhibits "dry wit," usually one-liners which can be sarcastic in nature.

Deep   Intense and often introspective with a distaste for surface conversation and pursuits.

15 Mediator   Consistently finds him- or herself in the role of reconciling differences in order to avoid conflict.

Musical   Participates in or has a deep appreciation for music, is committed to music as an art form, rather than the fun of performance.

	Mover	Driven by a need to be productive, is a leader whom others follow, finds it difficult to sit still.
	Mixes easily	Loves a party and can't wait to meet everyone in the room; never meets a stranger.
16	**Thoughtful**	A considerate person who remembers special occasions and is quick to make a kind gesture.
	Tenacious	Holds on firmly, stubbornly, and won't let go until the goal is accomplished.
	Talker	Constantly talking, generally telling funny stories and entertaining everyone around, feeling the need to fill the silence in order to make others comfortable.
	Tolerant	Easily accepts the thoughts and ways of others without the need to disagree with or change them.
17	**Listener**	Always seems willing to hear what you have to say.
	Loyal	Faithful to a person, ideal, or job, sometimes beyond reason.
	Leader	A natural born director, who is driven to be in charge, and often finds it difficult to believe that anyone else can do the job as well.
	Lively	Full of life, vigorous, energetic.
18	**Contented**	Easily satisfied with what he or she has, rarely envious.
	Chief	Commands leadership and expects people to follow.
	Chartmaker	Organizes life, tasks, and problem solving by making lists, forms or graphs.
	Cute	Precious, adorable, center of attention.
19	**Perfectionist**	Places high standards on him- or herself, and often on others, desiring that everything be in proper order at all times.
	Pleasant	Easygoing, easy to be around, easy to talk with.
	Productive	Must constantly be working or achieving, often finds it very difficult to rest.
	Popular	Life of the party and therefore much desired as a party guest.
20	**Bouncy**	A bubbly, lively personality, full of energy.
	Bold	Fearless, daring, forward, unafraid of risk.
	Behaved	Consistently desires to conduct him- or herself within the realm of what he or she feels is proper.

Balanced		Stable, middle of the road personality, not subject to sharp highs or lows.

WEAKNESSES

21 **Blank** — Shows little facial expression or emotion.

Bashful — Shrinks from getting attention, resulting from self-consciousness.

Brassy — Showy, flashy, comes on strong, too loud.

Bossy — Commanding, domineering, sometimes overbearing in adult relationships.

22 **Undisciplined** — Has a lack of order that permeates most every area of his or her life.

Unsympathetic — Finds it difficult to relate to the problems or hurts of others.

Unenthusiastic — Tends to not get excited, often feeling it won't work anyway.

Unforgiving — Has difficulty forgiving or forgetting a hurt or injustice done to him or her, apt to hold on to a grudge.

23 **Reticent** — Unwilling or struggles against getting involved, especially when situation is complex.

Resentful — Often holds ill feelings as a result of real or imagined offenses.

Resistant — Strives, works against, or hesitates to accept any other way but his or her own.

Repetitious — Retells stories and incidents to entertain you without realizing he or she has already told the story several times before, is constantly needing something to say.

24 **Fussy** — Insistent over petty matters or details, calling for a great attention to trivial details.

Fearful — Often experiences feelings of deep concern, apprehension or anxiousness.

Forgetful — Lack of memory which is usually tied to a lack of discipline and not bothering to mentally record things that aren't fun.

Frank — Straightforward, outspoken, and doesn't mind telling you exactly what he thinks.

25 **Impatient**   Finds it difficult to endure irritation or wait for others.

  Insecure   Apprehensive or lacks confidence.

  Indecisive   Finds it difficult to make any decision at all. (Not the personality that labors long over each decision in order to make the perfect one.)

  Interrupts   More of a talker than a listener, who starts speaking without even realizing someone else is already speaking.

26 **Unpopular**   Has intensity and demand for perfection that can push others away.

  Uninvolved   Has no desire to listen or become interested in clubs, groups, activities, or other people's lives.

  Unpredictable   May be ecstatic one moment and down the next, or willing to help but then disappears, or promises to come but forgets to show up.

  Unaffectionate Finds it difficult to verbally or physically demonstrate tenderness openly.

27 **Headstrong**   Insists on having his or her own way.

  Haphazard   Has no consistent way of doing things.

  Hard to please Has standards set so high that it is difficult to ever satisfy them.

  Hesitant   Slow to get moving and hard to get involved.

28 **Plain**   Has a middle-of-the-road personality without highs or lows and shows little, if any, emotion.

  Pessimistic   While hoping for the best, generally sees the down side of a situation first.

  Proud   Has great self-esteem and sees him- or herself as always right and the best person for the job.

  Permissive   Allows others (including children) to do as they please in order to keep from being disliked.

29 **Angered easily** Has a childlike flash-in-the-pan temper that expresses itself in tantrum style and is over and forgotten almost instantly.

  Aimless   Not a goal-setter, with little desire to be one.

  Argumentative   Incites arguments generally because he or she is right no matter what the situation may be.

  Alienated   Easily feels estranged from others, often because of insecurity or fear that others don't really enjoy his or her company.

30 Naive

Simple and child-like perspective, lacking sophistication or comprehension of what the deeper levels of life are really about.

Negative attitude

Has an attitude that is seldom positive and is often able to see only the down or dark side of each situation.

Nervy

Full of confidence, fortitude, and sheer guts, often in a negative sense.

Nonchalant

Easy-going, unconcerned, indifferent.

31 Worrier

Consistently feels uncertain, troubled, or anxious.

Withdrawn

Pulls back to him- or herself and needs a great deal of alone or isolation time.

Workaholic

Must be constantly productive and feels very guilty when resting, is not driven by a need for perfection or completion but by a need for accomplishment and reward, an aggressive goal-setter.

Wants credit

Thrives on the credit or approval of others. As an entertainer this person feeds on the applause, laughter, and/or acceptance of an audience.

32 Too sensitive

Overly introspective and easily offended when misunderstood.

Tactless

Sometimes expresses him- or herself in a somewhat offensive and inconsiderate way.

Timid

Shrinks from difficult situations.

Talkative

Entertaining, compulsive talker, finds it difficult to listen.

33 Doubtful

Feels uncertainty and lack of confidence that anything will ever work out.

Disorganized

Lacks ability to ever get life in order.

Domineering

Compulsively takes control of situations and/or people, usually telling others what to do.

Depressed

Feels down much of the time.

34 Inconsistent

Erratic, contradictory, with actions and emotions not based on logic.

Introvert

Thoughts and interest are directed inward, lives within him- or herself.

Intolerant

Appears unable to withstand or accept another's attitudes, point of view, or way of doing things.

Indifferent

Feels that most things don't matter one way or the other.

35 **Messy**   Lives in a state of disorder, unable to find things.

    Moody   Doesn't get very high emotionally, but easily slips into low lows, often when feeling unappreciated.

    Mumbles   Will talk quietly under the breath when pushed, doesn't bother to speak clearly.

    Manipulative   Influences or manages shrewdly or deviously for his or her own advantage, will get his or her way somehow.

36 **Slow**   Doesn't often act or think quickly, too much of a bother.

    Stubborn   Determined to exert his or her own will, not easily persuaded, obstinate.

    Show-off   Needs to be the center of attention, wants to be watched.

    Skeptical   Disbelieving, questioning the motive behind the words.

37 **Loner**   Requires a lot of private time and tends to avoid other people.

    Lord over others   Doesn't hesitate to let you know that he or she is right or is in control.

    Lazy   Evaluates work or activity in terms of how much energy it will take.

    Loud   Has a laugh or voice that can be heard above others in the room.

38 **Sluggish**   Slow to get started, needs push to be motivated.

    Suspicious   Tends to suspect or distrust others or ideas.

    Short-tempered   Has a demanding impatience-based anger and a short fuse. Anger is expressed when others are not moving fast enough or have not completed what they have been asked to do.

    Scatterbrained   Lacks the power of concentration, or attention, flighty.

39 **Revengeful**   Knowingly or otherwise holds a grudge and punishes the offender, often by subtly withholding friendship or affection.

    Restless   Likes constant new activity because it isn't fun to do the same things all the time.

    Reluctant   Unwilling or struggles against getting involved.

    Rash   May act hastily, without thinking things through, generally because of impatience.

40 **Compromising**   Will often relax his or her position, even when right, in order to avoid conflict.

Critical   Constantly evaluates and makes judgments, frequently thinks or expresses negative reactions.

Crafty   Shrewd, one who can always find a way to get to the desired end.

Changeable   Has a child-like, short attention span that needs a lot of change and variety to keep from getting bored.

An Overview of the Personalities

Popular Sanguines
"Let's do it the fun way"

Desire: have fun

Emotional needs: attention, affection, approval, acceptance

Key strengths: ability to talk about anything at any time at any place, bubbling personality, optimism, sense of humor, storytelling ability, enjoyment of people

Key weaknesses: disorganized, can't remember details or names, exaggerates, not serious about anything, trusts others to do the work, too gullible and naive

Get depressed when: life is no fun and no one seems to love them

Are afraid of: being unpopular or bored, having to live by the clock, having to keep a record of money spent

Like people who: listen and laugh, praise and approve

Dislike people who: criticize, don't respond to their humor, don't think they are cute

Are valuable in work for: colorful creativity, optimism, light touch, cheering up others, entertaining

Could improve if they: got organized, didn't talk so much, learned to tell time

As leaders they: excite, persuade, and inspire others; exude charm and entertain; are forgetful and poor on follow-through

Tend to marry: Perfect Melancholies who are sensitive and serious, but whom they quickly tire of having to cheer up and by whom they soon tire of being made to feel inadequate or stupid

Reaction to stress: leave the scene, go shopping, find a fun group, create excuses, blame others

Recognized by their: constant talking, loud volume, bright eyes

Powerful Cholerics
"Let's do it my way"

Desire: have control

Emotional needs: sense of obedience, appreciation for accomplishments, credit for ability

Key strengths: ability to take charge of anything instantly and to make quick, correct judgments

Key weaknesses: too bossy, domineering, autocratic, insensitive, impatient, unwilling to delegate or give credit to others

Get depressed when: life is out of control and people won't do thing their way

Are afraid of: losing control of anything (e.g., losing a job, not being promoted, becoming seriously ill, having a rebellious child or unsupportive mate)

Like people who: are supportive and submissive, see things their way, cooperate quickly, let them take credit

Dislike people who: are lazy and not interested in working constantly, buck their authority, become independent, aren't loyal

Are valuable in work because they: can accomplish more than anyone else in a shorter time, are usually right

Could improve if they: allowed others to make decisions, delegated authority, became more patient, didn't expect everyone to produce as they do

As leaders they have: a natural feel for being in charge, a quick sense of what will work, a sincere belief in their ability to achieve, a potential to overwhelm less aggressive people

Tend to marry: Peaceful Phlegmatics who will quietly obey and not buck their authority, but who never accomplish enough or get excited over their projects

Reaction to stress: tighten control, work harder, exercise more, get rid of the offender

Recognized by their: fast-moving approach, quick grab for control, self-confidence, restless and overpowering attitude

Perfect Melancholies
"Let's do it the right way"

Desire: have it right

Emotional needs: sense of stability, space, silence, sensitivity, support

Key strengths: ability to organize and set long-range goals, have high standards and ideals, analyze deeply

Key weaknesses: easily depressed, too much time on preparation, too focused on details, remembers negatives, suspicious of others

Get depressed when: life is out of order, standards aren't met, and no one seems to care

Are afraid of: no one understanding how they really feel, making a mistake, having to compromise standards

Like people who: are serious, intellectual, deep, and will carry on a sensible conversation

Dislike people who: are lightweights, forgetful, late, disorganized, superficial, prevaricating, and unpredictable

Are valuable in work for: sense of detail, love of analysis, follow-through, high standards of performance, compassion for the hurting

Could improve if they: didn't take life quite so seriously, didn't insist others be perfectionists

As leaders they: organize well, are sensitive to people's feelings, have deep creativity, want quality performance

Tend to marry: Popular Sanguines for their outgoing personality and social skills, but whom they soon attempt to quiet and get on a schedule

Reaction to stress: withdraw, get lost in a book, become depressed, give up, recount the problems

Recognized by their: serious and sensitive nature, well-mannered approach, self-deprecating comments, meticulous and well-groomed looks

Peaceful Phlegmatic
"Let's do it the easy way"

Desire: avoid conflict, keep peace

Emotional needs: sense of respect, feeling of worth, understanding, emotional support

Key strengths: balance, even disposition, dry sense of humor, pleasing personality

Key weaknesses: lack of decisiveness, enthusiasm, and energy; a hidden will of iron

Get depressed when: life is full of conflict, they have to face a personal confrontation, no one wants to help, the buck stops with them

Are afraid of: having to deal with a major personal problem, being left holding the bag, making major changes

Like people who: will make decisions for them, will recognize their strengths, will not ignore them, will give them respect

Dislike people who: are too pushy, too loud, and expect too much of them

Are valuable in work because they: mediate between contentious people, objectively solve problems

Could improve if they: set goals and became self-motivated, were willing to do more and move faster than expected, could face their own problems as well as they handle those of others

As leaders they: keep calm, cool, and collected; don't make impulsive decisions; are well-liked and inoffensive; won't cause trouble; don't often come up with brilliant new ideas

Tend to marry: Powerful Cholerics who are strong and decisive, but by whom they soon tire of being pushed around and looked down upon

Reaction to stress: hide from it, watch TV, eat, tune out life

Recognized by their: calm approach, relaxed posture (sitting or leaning when possible)

Appendix D

Comparison Chart
of Different Personality Systems

The Personalities	Popular Sanguine	Powerful Choleric	Perfect Melancholy	Peaceful Phlegmatic
Gary Smalley & John Trent	Otter	Lion	Beaver	Golden Retriever
DISC	Influencing/ Interacting	Dominance	Compliance/ Cautious	Steadiness
True Colors	Orange	Gold	Green	Blue
Alessandra & Cathcart	Socializer	Director	Thinker	Relater
Larry Crabb	Emotional	Volitional	Rational	Personal
Merrill-Reid Social Styles	Expressive	Driving	Analytical	Amiable

The Author

Marita Littauer is a professional speaker with over twenty-five years of experience speaking to women's groups, church conferences, conventions, and businesses. She is the author of thirteen books including *Personality Puzzle* and *Getting Along with Almost Anybody*. Marita is the president and cofounder of CLASServices Inc., an organization that provides resources, training, and promotion for speakers and authors. Marita and her husband Chuck Noon have been married since 1983. For more information on Marita and/or CLASS, please visit www.classervices.com or call 800-433-6633.